Baptism

Baptism

A User's Guide

EXPLORING CHRISTIAN FAITH

Martin E. Marty

Augsburg Books
MINNEAPOLIS

BAPTISM
A User's Guide

Unless otherwise identified, scripture quotations are from the New Revised Standard Version Bible, copyright © 1989 by the division of Christian Education of the National Council of the Churches of Christ in the USA. Used by permission. All rights reserved.

Cover art: Photo © Chase Swift / Corbis. Used by permission.
Cover design: Mudville Design
Interior design: PerfecType, Nashville, Tenn.

Library of Congress Cataloging-in-Publication Data

Marty, Martin E., 1928-
  Baptism : a user's guide / Martin E. Marty.
    p. cm. -- (Exploring Christian faith)
  Includes bibliographical references and index.
  ISBN 978-0-8066-8049-1 (alk. paper)
  1. Baptism. I. Title.

BV811.3.M37 2008
234'.161--dc22
                        2008031639

The paper used in this publication meets the minimum requirements of American National Standard for Information Sciences—Permanence of Paper for Printed Library Materials, ANSI Z329.48-1984.

Manufactured in the U.S.A.

12   11   10   09   08   1   2   3   4   5   6   7   8   9   10

To my Godchildren
Children of God

Contents

Introduction: "Using" Baptism:
A Word between You and Me   1

1. Using the Baptismal Sign of the Cross—Daily   5
2. The Dangerous Grace of Baptizing   12
3. Using the Faith Connected with Baptism   27
4. The Useful Gifts and Benefits of Baptism   41
5. Water Alone Is Useless in Baptism   73
6. The Significance of Baptism with Water   82
7. The Dangers and Rewards of Infant Baptism   89
8. Baptism and Faith—Faith and Baptism   95
9. User's Guide to Baptism   113
    To adults being baptized—and everyone else   114
    A letter for an infant being baptized—to be
       opened someday   122
    To you parents, of course   130
    A conversation with a child's godparents   136
    The gospel for the baptizer   140
    Words for the community that receives the baptized   145

Questions for Reflection and Discussion   157
Abbreviations   163
Index of Topics   164
Index of Biblical References   167

Introduction
"Using" Baptism:
A Word between You and Me

WHILE WE WERE PLANNING this book, the publisher and editor asked, "Are you writing primarily for adult baptized believers who want better to understand baptism or for the unbaptized who are considering baptism?"

A brisk answer could be, "Yes!" The book is intended for the baptized *and* the unbaptized. A more thoughtful answer would be that it is written for (a) the baptized who want to understand this sacrament better and to put it refreshingly to use all their lives, and it is also written for (b) the unbaptized who are considering baptism, with that hope that they will, as it were, read while looking over the shoulders of the (a) readers. The unbaptized can then picture what the consequences will be for them if they do present themselves for baptism and they can understand how they too might put baptism to work for the rest of their lives.

We can even picture readers in a (c) category—people of faiths other than Christian or of no faith at all. This book might help them understand why baptism, which probably looks to them like a mere splashing of water, is so important to believers throughout their lives. They will find why believers focus in faith on the divine words spoken during the baptismal event, and why the combination of water + Word amounts not to a magic act, mere custom, or a nice thing to do. This book will help such readers grasp why Christians experience the day of baptism (unremembered if it occurred in infancy) as, after a person's physical birth, the most decisive event in life.

The choice to focus on the already baptized might appear to be a market-driven decision. In cultures where the majority of people have been baptized, those who want to understand their baptism more deeply will make up the natural readership for a book such as this. Much as we might wish otherwise, the odds are not good that casual passers-by in libraries or bookstores will take this book off the shelf, given the many kinds of books bidding for their attention. More than considerations of the market and the size of the readership, however, went into the decision to focus this book on the already baptized. Let me explain.

I believe that many baptized believers sell the sacrament short when they neglect their baptism and all but forget about it. They are missing some of the delight that comes with this "means of grace," and missing a deeper understanding of what grace means. They will not be as aware as they might be of what "forgiveness of sins" can mean *for each day* when it is *connected each day* with baptism. They are also not likely to be able to tell enough about baptism to commend it to searchers and inquirers— (b) readers—who, with someone to tell them what it means, might learn to welcome the gifts of baptism and become a part of the global community of the baptized.

Readers may notice from the start that this book is a personal address to them. Already I have used personal pronouns such as "you" and "me," or "I" about ten times. Professors used to be trained to avoid such pronouns, to write with forced or mock humility as if they were looking at their subject and their readers from a distance. They were encouraged to refer to themselves as "the present writer," or something like that, all to avoid the use of "I." Such usage may fit in formal academic treatises, but since this book is designed for "users," it invites a more natural approach.

I, alias "the present writer," am also a pastor. Whether they preach, teach, write, counsel, or converse, pastors aim for the head *and* the heart, and are not afraid to use the language of "you" and "me." The choice of familiar language and an informal tone does *not* mean, however, that we will avoid those difficult themes (doctrinal issues) that the subject of baptism demands and merits. My goal of contributing to understanding will be out of reach if I do not do some justice to what biblical and later theological authors have set down about the meaning and use of baptism.

Some of *you* might question how heavy doctrinal and theological matters can find a place in a book whose very title sounds practical. The people we here call "users" are to make a habit of putting knowledge about baptism into daily practice. You are to "use" your knowledge. Readers of the gospels and the letters of the New Testament will find that the biblical authors, inspired by the Holy Spirit, talk or write about the "use" of the divine Word in daily life, whether in the face of doubt and temptation or in the onrush of grace and the experience of delight. So, among professors or pastors, writers or readers, the baptized or the unbaptized, individual searchers or Christians in classes, the word *use* is or should be an appropriate word, and we will use it.

1

Using the Baptismal Sign
of the Cross—Daily

YOU MAY HAVE DONE a dangerous but delightful thing this morning.

You may engage in doing it again tonight.

If you made the sign of the cross, you were making *use* of your baptism in a brief sacramental ceremony. You were venturing to keep a perilous commitment, but one filled with promise, while following a very simple two-line suggestion, one that comes close to being a command. Not all Christian traditions put the matter as we shall and not all adopt the external features of it, but here is how it goes in the lives and practice of millions:

> In the morning, as soon as you get out of bed, you are to make the sign of the holy cross and say: *Under the care of God the Father + Son, and Holy Spirit. Amen.* (LSC, 58)

Following this, the believer is given further directions of what to do while "kneeling or standing." It is evidently assumed that still-sleepy people should undertake some action to go with the words as they "say the Apostles' Creed and the Lord's Prayer." More modestly, the author of this ritual adds, "If you wish, you may recite this little prayer as well," and he then provides such a prayer. You are welcome to make use of this little formula, an act intended to change the day ahead of you.

That sample morning prayer, simple as it is, displays an awareness of the treacherous character of human life. If you speak or think its words you will be giving thanks to God "that you have protected me through the night from all harm and danger," and, looking ahead, asking that God "would also protect me today from sin and every danger."

While this prayer focuses on you, it is not uttered for simply selfish reasons. Instead you pray "that my life and actions may please you," God. Soon after praying you may head off into traffic to work or to pursue leisure activities, which also can represent dangers of various sorts. As you pray, aware of all kinds of danger, you say that you commend "my body, my soul, and all that is mine" to God. Then follows a stunner about the appropriate mood for any kind of day: "After singing a hymn, or whatever else may serve your devotion, you are to go to your work joyfully."

In the evening, a similar little rite closes the day, again with the "sign of the holy cross" and prayers. There is no suggestion this time that a person might sing a hymn. The one sung in the morning may have tested the patience of others who live in the house or next door. But again a surprising if quieter line ends the practice: "Then you are to go to sleep quickly and cheerfully."

We can pick apart everything said so far, and for experimental reasons, we shall do so, hoping that our examination matches thoughts that may have been gathering in your mind.

Saying a prayer in your private quarters sounds quiet, looks safe, and is far from where most dangers threaten. It therefore sounds showy, if not absurd, for me to observe and say that it is perilous.

If we follow the suggestion that we should make the sign of the holy cross on our body, we should do it while being well aware of the risks to the body. The gesture lends itself to superstitious concepts, or at least it may seem to invoke magic. Make the sign of the cross at the free-throw line in basketball, and if you make the basket, you can foolishly credit God and yourself for the special divine favor that made it possible.

Make the sign of the cross often enough and it can become merely mechanical. Make the sign of the cross without thinking of what it means and you may be invoking not God but magic. Since this gesture is eminently subject to misuse, anyone who uses it should be aware of the dangers that can go along with it.

Notice what ought to be obvious: we regard any uses of the sign of the cross that might be confused with magic or superstition as perilous to spiritual health. Still, because the recommendation for its use remains strong after centuries, serious Christians all along must have believed that the assets and positives of *thoughtfully* making the sign of the cross outweigh the possible negatives.

In these self-critical moments, we can take time to add some more skeptical questions to those already implied. Isn't it melodramatic to speak of the "harm and danger" that will assault you or everyone else every day and night? While most people on earth do lack the protection of locks, alarm systems, anti-terrorist agencies, and law officers, many who pray this prayer appear to be safe enough. They will have a list of things to do in the day that follows morning prayer. They may suffer all kinds of distractions that are admittedly minor, though these can still keep them from falling asleep at night. In the midst of such plans and distractions, why make the sign of the cross and pray?

Finally, what is jostling about the suggestion that we make the sign of the cross and pray is that, after doing these recommended motions and words, we are urged in the morning to "go to work joyfully," and at night to "go to sleep quickly and cheerfully." Most people who have found a job after having been unemployed will know and testify that work *can* be approached joyfully. Many of us really enjoy our work, are surrounded with good colleagues, and find fulfillment in our assignments and labors. But, realistically, joy is hard to find where work is backbreaking, as it is for hundreds of millions of sweat laborers. Joy is elusive when the boss is tyrannous, the competition is out to get you, the assembly line is soul-deadening, and your future is threatened by globalization, hostile corporate takeovers, cutbacks, and other forces beyond your control. Still, whatever the situation and the prospects of the day, we read that we are to go "joyfully." What does making the sign of the cross in order to signal the recall of baptism achieve? How does it enable us to go joyfully?

After completing a day of work as just described, how can you be told, with the implied assurance that it's possible, to "go to sleep quickly and cheerfully"? Making the sign of the cross and saying some prayers will not provide you with a cure for sleep disorders. It will not prevent the idled but uncontrolled brain of even contented persons from suffering nightmares, nor will it keep whole reels of mental images that deal with envisioned and worried-over bad tomorrows from running through your head.

Neither outcome—going to work joyfully nor going to sleep cheerfully—is natural for most people. Something other than "natural" has to be at issue. The phrase "something other than natural" calls to mind the supernatural, which in our culture usually suggests a commitment to superstition.

There are legitimate concerns about misuse of the sign of the cross and the prayers that leave us with this question: *Why?* Why invoke the sign of the cross at all and why say the prayers? Clearly, many Christians go through life never making the sign of the cross and they get along fine. Many Christians follow alternative rituals and habits, using signs designed to achieve what making the sign of the cross also sets out to do: to bring the meaning and effects of baptism to mind. These believers may even never have heard of making the sign of the cross and still their bodies and souls are protected by a provident God.

It is good to remind ourselves that making or not making the sign of the cross and that praying or not praying are external matters related to choices we may make. To engage in these two routines is utterly and emphatically unmagical; their use represents one choice among many, one act of many acts of personal devotion that can remind us of the gifts and promises of baptism.

That may all be true, but there has to be some positive reason for beginning this book with an accent on this daily routine. There remains, then, this question: what exactly do you signify with the sign of the cross and, along with it, those hymns and prayers? Answer: the whole process signifies *baptism*. It calls for and encourages the gift and grace of baptism to be used daily throughout life.

We would not have spent three lines, to say nothing of having given three pages, to this morning and evening practice did it not connect so closely with the commended daily use of baptism. The

one who made the connection in this case, and the one who recommended that we adopt this practice, was the ex-monk Martin
Luther. As is well known, Luther often pondered the meaning
and the role of each day as it was experienced in the life of the
baptized. We could have cited any number of other figures in
Christian history to press this point, but Luther's purpose and
prescription commend themselves as being particularly clear.

The monk was a professor of the Hebrew Scriptures, the Old
Testament and, more notably, a preacher also of the New. He was
a biblical scholar who had in mind, and had often enough talked
about, a biblical theme that pointed to a particular moment in
the baptismal ceremony. It was that moment, to use contemporary wording, when the presiding minister marks the sign of
the cross on the forehead of each of the baptized. As the sign of
the cross is made, the minister says, "(Name), child of God, you
have been sealed by the Holy Spirit and marked with the cross of
Christ forever."

With such a seal and mark upon the body, an act to be
remembered and revisited by making the sign of the cross each
morning and each evening all through life, a baptized Christian
is reminded that he is a "child of God." Children in Christian
traditions that do not baptize anyone before reaching "the age
of reason" can reason that each of them, too, is a "child of God."
Those who baptize not only adults but also infants, however, find
special reasons to reinforce the awareness among everyone that
each baptized person is a child of God.

This "user's guide to baptism" begins, as does the day, with
the sign of the cross, and this chapter ends, as does the same day,
with the assurance that each believer who begins and ends each
day with the recollection of her baptism will be constantly aware
that she is a child of God, with all the rights and privileges—and

responsibilities—that go with being such a privileged person. *How* one is made a child of God will be made more clear as we go deeper into the background and meanings of baptism.

Whether one chooses to make the sign of the cross in remembrance of baptism or has some other way of daily recalling his baptism, it is good to remember that such acts of devotion connect with the call that goes back to the New Testament itself: you are to repent. Without repentance, there is no way for the conscientious Christian who is aware of the God of holiness to face the new day without being haunted by the past. Without repentance, there is no way to fall asleep at night quickly and in peace without having to deny the flaws and failures of the same day. "Repent and be baptized!" was John the Baptist's call. "Be baptized and repent!" is a way of continuing in the Christian life.

The mere mention of repentance can perhaps lead some to think that we are talking about something gloomy, even depressing. While confronting your soul (your self) in repentance can involve pain (we are not likely to be eager to admit our faults), the release that comes with divine forgiveness is exhilarating. In the gospels, repentance is regularly associated with *joy*. Jesus compared himself to the bridegroom at a wedding and asked why the groomsmen gathered at the table were so dreary. He stressed that being freed of sin is a joyful reality, so we do well to think not of the gloom but of the joy of repentance.

One question remains and awaits comment. Why, given the great promise that goes with baptismal grace, did we in the first two lines of this chapter say that, given the promise of baptism, it is dangerous to sign the cross and say the prayers in such a context? We will address that now.

2

The Dangerous Grace of Baptizing

A QUICK REVIEW of formal church ceremonies for the sacrament of baptism—still being used two thousand years after it was commanded and celebrated today in thousands of churches—leads us to examine one of them. This can be risky business. If I do not state the issue clearly, I might lead a reader considering whether to be baptized, or who is in the process of being prepared for baptism, to think twice after reading a formal order of baptism.

Parents and other guardians who are preparing to present a child for baptism could also stumble for a moment. Let's face it, the child *is not being asked* whether he is ready to make a commitment. If these adults think about it, they might feel a kind of terror as they think of the commitments and responsibility of care that *they* are undertaking.

In the opening part of one baptismal service, the portion called Presentation, the people we have just pictured will hear that the baptized person will be "joined in God's mission for the life of the world." A different service book puts it another way: the baptized, young or old, are to "grow in faith, love, and obedience to the will of God." This is heady stuff. It is possible that in many congregational settings, worshipers have heard such words so often that they lose the power to shock and inspire. If they listen closely, they will also be startled to hear that baptism means joining the one baptized "to the death and resurrection of our Lord Jesus Christ."

Baptism and martyrdom

To get an idea of what such joining means, it is urgent that we call to mind the fact that through the ages millions of the baptized, because they were joined to the death of Jesus Christ, were put to death. One wonders whether in our own time the parents who bring infants to be baptized or adults who respond to God's call to be baptized have any idea what the "mission" and "obedience to the will of God" might have meant for so many and what it might mean for us today. We call many of those who have gone before "witnesses" or martyrs and we attempt to live from their example. Later generations are sometimes made aware of the actual good that martyrs achieved in the face and under the weight of unimaginably evil forces for whom their baptism was offensive.

Through the centuries, numberless Christians have been put to death because they were baptized and *lived* the baptismal faith. In the sixteenth century, after the Jesuits brought baptismal faith to southern Japan, many thousands of Japanese accepted the promise of its gifts and benefits. For a variety of reasons, the political and religious climate suddenly changed. These new Christians were put in jeopardy and eventually many were killed for their faith. It turns out that Imperial leaders were threatened by the growing presence of citizens who were loyal to a new "Lord" and professed a higher allegiance to things of the Spirit. By being baptized, these Japanese became members of a community that the emperor, his courts, and the military could not tolerate. The Christians were called to recant their confessions of faith and repudiate their baptism.

In museums today we can still see some objects that indicate the scope of the purge. Among them you can find flat, metal icons of the virgin Mary and Jesus, some scraped and worn to the point his or her image is almost scratched away. These icons are called *fumie,* from the Japanese words for "picture" and "to step on," "stomp on," or "trample on." Why are they scraped and worn? The oppressors forced recanting Christians to prove that they meant their denial of the faith by trampling on the face of Mary or Jesus. Imagine how many thousands of trampling feet it took to cause such extreme marring and to create such deep grooves in the metal. Records of the time also show, however, that many baptized Christians remained faithful, considering their baptism to be indelible, its promises irremovable, its compensations valuable. They were aware of God's promises, which no amount of suffering and persecution could remove.

That was long ago. Today, experts who collect data on Christian trends tell us of several hundred thousand martyrdoms occurring annually around the globe. Only a few of those killed make the headlines—for example, when missionaries from the West take radical risks and try to convert Muslims right under the noses and watchful gaze of other Muslims. Strategically their work may seem to be foolish. Foolhardy missionaries are embarrassing to their governments and costly to their supporters. They may not provide the best illustrations of Christian good sense, but they do indicate how seriously some take the baptismal commitment.

In communist East Germany during the Cold War, repressive atheist officials did all they could to discourage the practice of Christian faith. While they could not prevent all grandparents from presenting their grandchildren for baptism, they could and did impose strictures on adults for participating in catechetical and confirmation classes. Such atheist regimes understood the power of baptism and confirmation as being so attractive that they came up with alternative ceremonies of "initiation" and "confirmation." These were generally bleak and somber parodies of Christian rites. They were psychologically necessary, however, because the official repression of the Christian sacraments and sacramentally committed citizens forced those officials to push parallel rites that did not mention God or witness to Christ.

Baptism and family tensions

Closer to home, and disturbing to family members in some religiously mixed marriages, there are many who suffer from the family tensions that come with the baptism of an adult convert or the bringing of a child to baptism. If mishandled, and even when well handled, the occasion can be at least temporarily destructive of family harmony and may haunt gatherings of relatives for a generation and more. Thus in many of the hundreds of thousands of marriages between Jews and Christians, the choice by a couple to have a child baptized or, more tensely, the demand by half a couple to bring a child to baptism, can be the most challenging disruption of marital "cease-fires" or "let's-just-get-along" situations.

The point here is not to resolve the "should haves" or "how-tos" that go into such decisions, but rather to show that in many cases families recognize how sharp and stark are the lines one crosses when there is a baptism and when the baptized and/or their families have firm commitments to and understandings of what is going on.

Calling these domestic acts of witness and the resulting difficulties to mind is a good exercise in realism. It confronts every worshiping congregation with a bracing new call to discipleship by Jesus Christ on baptismal day. Something important, something serious is happening—the one baptized and the baptized who watch the ceremony are called to daily discipleship. That's risky business.

The festivity matters but don't let it mask the danger

We moderns may properly do as many things as possible to make the sacramental ceremony and accompanying festivities as attractive as possible. In the case of infants, we can be quite sure that in middle-class families, a dress or suit, usually white, one that has been treasured through the generations or newly sewn or purchased at some expense, will be glorious. Whoever has witnessed baptismal rites in small Latin American village churches or among the poor in Africa or in U.S. cities will retain images of families and neighbors wearing festive clothes and will recall echoes of joyous music that stirred the souls of relatives on the happy day. Good. Let it all reflect the beauty of holiness that is to come with baptism.

Those who follow the baptism in church with a family gathering at home follow a tradition that goes back to biblical times, when such celebrations often included a feast with fatted calf and good wine. For those who are well off, the celebration might be quite elaborate, with the best dishes and fine linen. For others it might be a backyard barbeque. In the humblest peasant settings, among the poor of the world who by far make up the largest number of baptized celebrators, great care goes into trimming the bushes on the lawn for the ceremony when a church is too small to hold the gathered clan. Aunts and sometimes uncles who cook will prepare a worthy spread for the after-service festivities. Beautiful it all is, and no one should take anything away from it.

Viewed from another angle, however, it is important to understand that the satin of a child's baptismal dress, the sound of an organ or choir or congregational music, and the purity of the tablecloths for the dinner at home can easily become masks that can lead people to forget: *this ceremony is dangerous* because it is also grounded in and related to two deaths.

Jesus' death and our death

One death is that of Jesus Christ, since baptism occurs "in the name of the Father *and of the Son* and of the Holy Spirit." In the Presentation we are told that, "in baptism our gracious Father who frees us from sin and death" does so "by joining us to the death . . . of our Lord Jesus Christ."

It may look like cheating to use three periods in that sentence to cover the two words after "death," namely, "and resurrection." We know the outcome of his story—resurrection—and are joined to that outcome through baptismal faith. Realizing that, however, does not mean that the person being baptized will not experience various versions of the suffering that went with Christ's life and death and goes with our life and death as well.

On the day of baptism, other dangers loom than those that, in extraordinary days and ways, often led to physical death and martyrdom. Being joined by baptism to Jesus Christ's death can mean that along life's way circumstances could occur that might prompt us to cry out as he did from the cross: "My God, my God, why have you forsaken me?" That question remains the most memorable and haunting cry among those the gospels tell us he uttered while he was dying on the cross.

Imagine the countless Christians in numberless ICU units, deathbeds, battlefields, or scenes of violent activity and accidents in which they feel cut off from the protection for which they have prayed or the resurrection that is promised. Having prayed for protection as a baptized child of God and then experiencing seeming abandonment by God, alienation from dear ones, or isolation in the prison or sick room can put a strain on any believer. It all started with the dangerous activity of being identified with Jesus' cross in baptism.

The grace that comes with baptismal faith, however, reaches beyond places of physical danger and the spiritual confusions and enigmas they bring with them. An internal, bone-deep, soul-searing experience can afflict those who feel distanced at times from God, or who are facing a great temptation, or are actually straying into disobedience. But according to the New Testament, baptism as a means of grace identifies one with the God of grace who is present in all—even unhappy—circumstances. Therefore, for believers who daily mark their bodies with the sign of the cross (whether with external gestures or not), promising to be obedient no matter where temptation, failure, or success—yes, success, too!—leads them, their act represents a kind of dare to the self to remain steadfast. That virtual dare sounds—and is—dangerous, however ultimately rewarding the wager and commitment that come with baptism can be.

Desire and danger

Also part of the Presentation in the baptismal service is a question such as, "Called by the Holy Spirit, trusting the grace and love of God, *do you desire to be baptized into Christ?*" It is of course impossible for the newborn to "desire" baptism or to formulate and give voice to an answer. In the case of babies, who in many parts of the world make up the largest company of those who are baptized, the question is relayed to adults who represent the infant: *"Do you desire to have your child (or children) baptized?"* Those who present children for baptism are a part of the dangerous complex of baptismal activities. The believing community, made up on the one hand of two billion believers and on the other hand by a congregation and a family or circle of responsible friends, is making a statement that implies, "If this infant is represented as 'desiring' something, we ourselves who are part of his life had better seek the grace to follow through with him."

Trust and danger

The word *trust* comes up in connection with baptism. Whoever has taken seriously the concept of trust and trusting may beam and smile because of the honor that comes with the role of parent, sponsor, or godparent, but underneath it all a thoughtful and conscientious person should shudder to hear a sample of the commitments that usually get mentioned next. The "parents or others" are "entrusted"—*entrusted!*, that's dangerous!—with responsibilities, best spelled out and reproduced in the lines that follow here:

> *to live with [the children] among God's faithful people,*
> *bring them to the word of God and the holy supper,*

teach them the Lord's Prayer, the Creed, and the Ten
    Commandments,
place in their hands the holy scriptures,
and nurture them in faith and prayer
so that [the] children may learn to trust God,
proclaim Christ through word and deed,
care for others and the world God made,
and work for justice and peace. (FLW, 228)

Without doubt, many parents, godparents, sponsors, and the congregation—whose members are also asked to make promises—make these commitments sincerely. Some of them steadfastly follow through, and not a few mature Christians can testify to what it meant for them to have such adults pray for them, have fun with them, counsel them, and keep the commitments just mentioned. However, calendars and schedules for most people being what they are, human nature being what it is, and distractions being so frequent, for many the commitment wanes by the time the christening dinner, picnic, or fast food stop has ended. Sadly, these dangerous commitments for care are often jettisoned and forgotten a year or decades later.

Profession of faith and danger

Then follows another part of the event that has to be labeled "dangerous." It used to be a separate ceremony called "Exorcism." An unnerving shadow of it remains in even the polite company that gathers for baptisms within exquisite sanctuaries. It brings in to the sphere of stained-glass windows and sacred space some ominous characters and events such as "the devil and all the forces that defy God," "the powers of this world that rebel against God," and "the ways of sin that draw you from God." So brutal are such references that baptizers often hurry past them, but to do justice to the benefits of baptism we will explore them later.

Thanksgiving at the font

All the life of the believer is to be one of thanksgiving. Life and breath and all that surrounds the baptized are undeserved gracious gifts of God. Whoever realizes that does not want to be an ingrate and will want to "return thanks." So the baptismal ceremony, in calling for the giving of thanks, now centers on a theme and an act that we need not call risky, dangerous, or perilous.

The believing community from the beginning has associated the other sacrament, the Lord's Supper or "Holy Communion," with giving thanks. Now here also, in a typical order of service for a baptism, that note of gratitude appears. In a beautiful short text, the assembled baptizing company receives a reassuring history lesson. For all the hazards that follow baptism in the lives of all believers, we are here reminded that in the past God's people have had many occasions to give thanks.

And for what does one give thanks? In the Lord's Supper, often called the *Eucharist*, which means "thanksgiving," the subjects of thanks are bread and wine, sacramentally the body and blood of Jesus Christ, and then the spiritual circumstances of the believers, their mission, and the like.

In a baptismal service, where God works through the divine Word and through water, the mention of other waters also elicits gratitude. Let me quote a paragraph from an order of worship that gets us close to, drenched in, and then delivered from water:

> *We give you thanks, O God, for in the beginning your Spirit moved over the waters and by your Word you created the world, calling forth life in which you took delight. Through*

the waters of the flood you delivered Noah and his family, and through the sea you led your people Israel from slavery into freedom. At the river your Son was baptized by John and anointed with the Holy Spirit. By the baptism of Jesus' death and resurrection you set us free from the power of sin and death and raise us up to live in you.

Then follows what we might call a watery prayer of thanks:

Pour out your Holy Spirit, the power of your living Word, that those who are washed in the waters of baptism may be given new life. To you be given honor and praise through Jesus Christ our Lord, in the unity of the Holy Spirit, now and forever. (ELW, 230)

Reproducing these words, especially the reference to the death and resurrection of Jesus Christ, is intended to stress once more the dangerous side of the baptismal response and commitment. Whether we hear and think about these words on a once-in-a-lifetime day of baptism or in our daily devotional practice at home, the words do their job of connecting the baptized with the death of Jesus Christ. Notice, however, that all the occasions in which that deathly connection is made are also assertions of the power of Jesus' resurrection and the joy the believer receives by this identification with Christ and the benefits he brings.

While deferring detailed comment on the water for now, we will ponder the Word, especially its themes of creation, rescue, and resurrection. God "took delight" in creation, in which waters played such a part. God delivered Noah and company and freed slaves out of Egypt. It is not dangerous, but it is invigorating to find that the God in whose name we baptize was through the ages and is now a deliverer and agent of freedom. God the Holy Spirit was present at and in the baptism of Jesus. Even Jesus' death and resurrection are called a "baptism" because God, through this event, frees us and raises us up to live in him. New life follows from God, so honor and praise flow back to him from us. It is well when some of those mornings after a believer uses the sign of the cross and says a prayer that there follows a reading of scriptures that stress these positive themes, especially those associated with the resurrection.

The baptism itself by immersion, pouring, or sprinkling

When the service book with which I am most familiar directs the presiding minister to proceed, the language for what follows is in the passive voice: "The candidate *is immersed* in water, or water *is poured* on the candidate's head. . . ."

Some might reasonably think at this point that the Baptists and other Christian kin in their camp have it over the rest of us in one important respect. They always immerse the one being baptized. Of course, the rest of us do not have to believe that baptism by immersion works effects that other forms of baptism do not. The symbolism of putting the baptized one all the way under water, however, is certainly one way of making more vivid and picturesque one particular image in the apostle Paul's writings— being buried with Christ through baptism (Romans 6:4; Colossians 2:12). The act of immersing dramatically reinforces the idea that we should connect the words *baptism* and *danger*.

Some of us who can remember being pushed into water over our heads before we had learned to swim have no trouble thinking of immersion as perilous. Whoever has had to be rescued from deep waters for any reason—perhaps because he had gotten separated from his "buddy" co-swimmer, or because she stepped off an unforeseen ledge into deep waters, or because he fell over-board into the night and its threatening waters—knows what risk and trauma are. To come up from the waters is to experience release, relief, and *new life* itself.

Although we are not likely to see baptism by immersion spread among most Christians, we can at least point to it in order to ponder it. We can empathize with the plunged-under candidates, and we can picture the ways in which that safeguarded but still scary dunking goes on in a tank in a church or in a river. Survivors are lifted up and out, and then identified in symbolic ways with the resurrection. The rest of us either remember or imagine our way back from the font and the feeling of a few drops of water applied by "pouring" or "sprinkling." This is just as theologically valid as immersion, but is rather less picturesque.

After the commanded use of water, the newly baptized and thus freshly resurrected person (or his or her representatives) hears the endangering word on which we have been dwelling. It is endangering because it focuses on the fact that the new Christian is called to be a disciple of Jesus. Be the baptized one an adult or a child, the words applied are the same: *"Child of God, you have been sealed by the Holy Spirit and marked with the cross of Christ forever."*

Welcome

Since the believing and covenanted community made up of responsible adults has for these minutes been the deputy on the scene for Jesus Christ, this community or congregation receives a last word and gesture. These are often accompanied by the presentation of a lighted candle and some words about being a light and about letting the light shine as people go forth, carrying their symbolic lights, which stand for "the mission we share." The darkness might threaten, but it has not overcome "the Light of the World." The dangers in that surrounding darkness remain, but now there is a lighted force posed against it, carried in the hands of the baptized or, in the case of a child, of her representatives. The one baptized is then welcomed by the community of faith both into the congregation and into the mission God has given to God's people.

Postscript on externals

It is hard to resist, and I will not resist, the impulse to append a word by Martin Luther to these comments on the dangerous commitments that come with the reception of grace in baptism or the act of bringing someone to be baptized. Quoting Luther serves to debunk the idea that once upon a time everyone was well aware of the precariousness of their situation.

Luther wrote a Baptismal Booklet in which he berated congregants for the "carelessness and lack of solemnity—to say nothing of out and out levity" with which they treated the Sacrament of Baptism. He blamed some of the casual manner he observed on ignorance. This is why he proposed using ordinary language, not church Latin, in the ceremony. Aware of the dangers of laxity, he wrote expositions of the sacrament and felt called to comment: "It is no joke at all."

In the booklet, Luther added a caution, as we must, against confusing the externals of baptism with what was essential. We learn of a whole catalog of practices associated with baptism in his day, most of which are forgotten or have been reduced to minor roles in our own baptismal ceremonies.

Bear in mind, too, that in Baptism the external ceremonies are least important, such as blowing under the eyes, making the sign of the cross, putting salt in the mouth or spit and clay in the ears and nose, anointing the breast and shoulders with oil, smearing the head with chrism, putting on the christening robe, placing a burning candle in the child's hand, whatever else has been added by humans to embellish Baptism. For certainly a baptism can occur without any of these things, and they are not the proper device from which the devil shrinks or flees. He sneers at even greater things than these! Here things must get really serious. . . .

For this reason it is right and proper not to allow drunken and boorish pastors to baptize nor to select loose people as godparents. (LSC, 78-79)

Luther calls us to "get really serious" by getting beyond the externals. To get inside the subject, to discern the theological and practical meanings of baptism, a simple-seeming book, Martin Luther's Small Catechism, will provide a framework.

3

———— ✤ ————

Using the Faith Connected
with Baptism

NOT ALL CHRISTIANS conceive of the Sacrament of Baptism
in the same way. While our present conversation deals with baptism as it is understood by Christians who baptize infants *and*
adults, many millions of Christians do not baptize infants. They
are not to be overlooked or slighted, since their practices have
some things to teach the infant-baptizing churches. In terms of
this book, such Christians make different uses of baptism. Therefore members of churches who baptize people of all ages should
say, "Welcome to the conversation, all Baptists, Anabaptists,
members of Churches of Christ, Mennonites, Hutterites, Breth-
ren, Dunkers, and all the rest. We share Christian faith, but with
different understandings. Let's talk."

By overhearing the present conversation, which concerns the witness and practice of Lutheran, Catholic, Orthodox, Anglican, and most non-Baptist Protestants, *you* who baptize only adults can discern what understandings *we* bring to baptism. To prevent confusion, we will take up first this "catholic" or "liturgical" company of Christian churches, reserving talk about "believer's baptism" (often called "credobaptism") for later. (The historic but now seldom used name for the understanding of baptism in this book is "pedobaptist" or, in older spellings, "paedobaptism"—*paido* being the Greek word for "child.")

Most churches in this tradition use catechisms to define, instruct, and explain basic teachings, and to prepare people for baptism. Thus the new *Catechism of the Catholic Church*, a church that observes seven sacraments, defines baptism as "the first and chief sacrament of forgiveness of sins because it unites us with Christ, who died for our sins and rose for our justification." This definition goes on to detail the various modes of baptism, whether by immersion or pouring, but mentioning such details only serves to enhance the simple sentence about forgiveness of sins and the uniting of the believer with Christ. Most Protestants would be glad to include that Catholic definition in their understanding of baptism, and many of them do.

Secondly, "An Outline of the Faith Commonly Called the Catechism" is included in the Episcopal *Book of Common Prayer*. Its definition is also briskly stated:

Q. What is Holy Baptism?

A. Holy Baptism is the sacrament by which God adopts us as his children and makes us members of Christ's Body, the Church, and inheritors of the kingdom of God. (PBH, 858)

A match for these, but one that does not begin with what becomes its central theme, "forgiveness of sins," is in Martin Luther's Small Catechism, memorized by catechumens in many languages through almost five centuries:

> What is Baptism?
>
> Answer: Baptism is not simply plain water. Instead it is water used according to God's command and con-nected with God's word.

Luther, being Luther, has to certify his answer with a biblical reference:

> What then is the Word of God?
>
> Answer: Where our Lord Jesus Christ says in Mat-thew 28:19, "Go therefore and make disciples of all nations, baptizing them in the name of the Father and of the Son and of the Holy Spirit." (LSC, 40)

The spelling out of the benefits and uses of the sacrament appears a couple of lines later in Luther's Catechism, as it stresses the role of God's Word, which sets this water aside for special use.

Those three definitions, and others current among the East-ern Orthodox and most Protestant groups, appear in contexts in which some different nuances as well as more serious differences of doctrinal understanding appear. However, all these church bod-ies refuse to "re-baptize" anyone who has been baptized with water "in the name of the Father and of the Son and of the Holy Spirit."

Taking the first and basic lines of almost any church body's definition of baptism would hardly satisfy a questioner who wants to know what it all means. The older Catechism definitions were written from within intact "Christian cultures," which means that the public would retain some understanding of what was going on in baptism because churchgoers among them would regularly see and hear baptism talked about. If one lived in Spain, the talk heard and ceremonies seen would deal with Catholic interpretations. In England, the privileged Anglican Church set the terms, just as in Switzerland, the Reformed interpretation prevailed, or in Sweden, the Lutheran. In most of those cultures, virtually everyone was baptized in and into the Christian church through the ministry of the particular dominating communion. Non-church goers could look out the window or down the street and see families heading for the cathedral or chapel and later to the inn or family table. Of course, in such surroundings, a great deal of folk custom became a part of baptisms.

Where one form of Christianity was privileged and prevailed, a believer did not face what today's Christians confront, namely, societies called "secular" and "pluralist." One has to start from scratch to explain particular forms and meanings of baptism and baptism itself in such cultures.

So a Christian in one or another of the baptizing communions gets asked today, "What is baptism?" In order to do some justice to the question when answering it, the respondent who reaches into a historical and biblical tradition might answer with more detail than the busy questioner desired to learn. In outline, he would point to the background of baptism in the Hebrew Scriptures and in the world around Jesus and his disciples, where varieties of water ceremonies were practiced. Jesus and the disciples did not invent them. After the resurrection and Pentecost, as the Christian community developed, many religions were at home in the Roman Empire. Some of them displayed Greek influence in their rites of initiation, which often included washings or immersions. To be realistic, the questioner who asks "What is baptism?" would likely regard talk about Rome and Greece as a diversion that will not help her decide whether to be baptized or what it would mean for her child.

The impatience of a busy questioner can be addressed for the moment by a believer who comes quickly to the point and turns to the gospels. There baptism is lifted up and highlighted in the accounts of John, who is called the Baptist. John, who called Israel to repent, was always seen as the prophetic forerunner of Jesus. In those gospel accounts, before John baptized Jesus, he seemed puzzled, bemused, or even put off by Jesus' presentation of himself at the waters for baptism. John had consistently and vigorously taught that *his baptism was for forgiveness*, while Jesus, of course, is pictured as having no sins to be forgiven.

What sense did it make then for Jesus to be baptized? In the gospel accounts, Jesus gives an answer that suggests that he is identified with needy humanity, and that he is baptized to make his identification with sinners complete. Still the gospel picture of baptism is not filled in at that point. John elaborates a bit when he prophesies that Jesus will baptize with the Spirit, but not with water.

Once again, we picture an inquirer saying, "Get to the point." What does John the Baptist's baptisms have to do with that of my niece? It is a good question. Whoever feels the burden of sin, or seeks faith by being baptized, or renewal by revisiting in repentance her own baptism, which occurred years before, will begin to make a connection.

In his preaching and counsel, Jesus uses baptism in some cases as a metaphor by referring to it as suffering. Such talk is a reminder that baptism, for all its graces and delights, is in its own way dangerous, because it is so easily and regularly related to suffering. Here is a dramatic instance: in Mark 10:39, Jesus explicitly uses this image of suffering: "The cup that I drink you will drink; and with the baptism with which I am baptized, you will be baptized." If your Bible has footnotes, you might find one that stresses that the acceptance of baptism, in this usage, means acceptance of God's way—a way that, given the way the world is, might well lead to suffering or even death. These words of Jesus in the gospel color our understandings of baptism and show how dramatic and decisive any talk about it has to be.

As important as forgiveness and entrance into the kingdom and becoming disciples were, there are not many gospel stories about baptism. Jesus himself does not baptize anyone. In the fourth chapter of the Fourth Gospel there is one mention of his disciples baptizing. The Pharisees, we are told, had heard, "Jesus is making and baptizing more disciples than John"—but the evangelist quickly adds, "although it was not Jesus himself but his disciples who baptized" (John 4:1-2). To this point, the contemporary who asks "What is baptism?" gets only bits and pieces of an answer, and few of them inform today's questioner about central meanings of the sacrament, until . . .

Until after Jesus' resurrection, where there is a startling report in virtually the last line of Mark, usually thought of as the oldest surviving gospel. There is another astonishing report near the end of Matthew, another text that later Christians enshrined and try to follow.

The endings of Mark and Matthew

Most scholars, including many conservatives, believe that the last page of Mark in most printed Bibles was not part of the original text. In it there is a strong reference from the mouth of the resurrected Lord: "Go into all the world and proclaim the good news to the whole creation. The one who believes and is baptized will be saved; but the one who does not believe will be condemned" (Mark 16:15-16).

The same scholars—and most of the faithful—though aware of the words in Mark, have made more of the ending of Matthew. It is the heavyweight among the references, the charge that has led missionaries to go to places all over the globe. This text, which has inspired evangelizing efforts everywhere, is one that Luther saw as the root of Christian response to an urgent divine command. We read that just before Jesus parted from his disciples, an act which removed his bodily presence:

> Jesus came and said to them, "All authority in heaven and on earth has been given to me. Go therefore and make disciples of all nations, baptizing them in the name of the Father and of the Son and of the Holy Spirit, and teaching them to obey everything that I have commanded you. And remember, I am with you always, to the end of the age." (Matthew 28:18-20)

To many critical scholars, this ending is so forceful, neat, and precise that it could be a later insertion into the Jesus story by the emerging church. While that kind of criticism can never be addressed decisively, the command is so anchored in the biblical canon and the memory and response of believers through twenty centuries that it will remain the charter for baptizers. No matter how often some scholars have seen it as a later insertion, it has survived and will remain the foundation for a basic and powerful Christian practice and teaching—baptism.

Baptism in the book of Acts

The book of Acts, an account of early Christianity written by the author of the Gospel of Luke, shows more evidence of baptism's central role in the work and ways and words of the apostles. The book begins with a flashback to the forty days during which the

resurrected Lord was, on occasion, experienced as present among
the disciples. The reference appears in a passage in which Jesus
foresaw the coming of the Holy Spirit on Pentecost. This event
is called "the promise of the Father." The promise? Jesus said,
"This . . . is what you have heard from me; for John baptized with
water, but you will be baptized with the Holy Spirit not many
days from now" (1:4-5).

The book of Acts is a kind of history of the spread of Christianity that occurred through the awakening of faith and the
instrument of baptism. Its stories help anyone who is trying
to stammer out on biblical grounds an answer to the question:
"What is baptism?" First off, Peter preached an eloquent Pentecost sermon that "cut to the heart" of the crowd, which there-
upon asked him and the other apostles, "Brothers, what should
we do?" Peter said to them, "Repent, and be baptized every one
of you in the name of Jesus Christ so that your sins may be forgiven; and you will receive the gift of the Holy Spirit" (2:37-38).
The people responded enthusiastically, for "those who welcomed
his message were baptized, and that day about three thousand
persons were added" (2:41).

An outline of a sequence emerges in the pages of Acts: (1)
repent, (2) be baptized, (3) thus be forgiven, (4) receive the gift of
the Holy Spirit, and (5) be "added" to the company of the apostles.
The catechisms stick to the main point when they relate baptism
to both forgiveness and community.

The eighth chapter of Acts is crammed with such references.
One Simon, a magician who had attracted a crowd, was upstaged
by an evangelist named Philip, who was "proclaiming the good
news about the kingdom of God and the name of Jesus Christ."
The author reports that after Philip's teaching, "they were baptized,
both men and women" (8:12). If baptism's roots were in part on

both inherited and still contemporary Judaism, with its practice of circumcision for all men and boys, now among the followers of Jesus baptizing was to be for everyone—women included. Ever after that first generation, the formula from Matthew seems to have been operative, and baptism occurred regularly and decisively "in the name of the Father and of the Son and of the Holy Spirit."

Picking up on Jesus' word about going into "all nations," and setting out to demonstrate that the kingdom was to go far beyond the narrow confines of Israel, the author of Acts told the story of a eunuch who had been in Jerusalem to worship but was now heading home to Ethiopia, where he was an official. After Philip explained a prophetic text to him as "good news" and applied it to Jesus, the visitor spotted some water along the way and asked, "What is to prevent me from being baptized?" Philip and the eunuch went down into the water "and Philip baptized him" (8:38).

A startling extension of baptismal work came when Saul, who later described himself as the major persecutor of believers, was struck blind by a flashing light and stunned by the questioning voice of the resurrected Jesus. He later had his sight restored by a disciple named Ananias. Saul was baptized and, to signify the beginning of his new life, he was named Paul, and he became a great apostle (9:18).

The disciple Peter was also busy, as Acts describes it, preaching and converting the whole household of a Gentile soldier named Cornelius at Caesarea. After seeing that God's Spirit was at work in the household, it was Peter the apostle who asked, "Can anyone withhold the water for baptizing these people who have received the Holy Spirit just as we have?" No one could, so he ordered them to be "baptized in the name of Jesus Christ"

(10:47-48). When Peter became a new convert to the cause of reaching Gentiles and including them in the company of believers, he defended his action, this time quoting "the word of the Lord." He recalled how Jesus had said, "John baptized with water, but you will be baptized with the Holy Spirit" (11:16). So they were baptized. Their *repentance* was a key element in this revelation of an expanding mission.

The scope was enlarged further when, still according to Acts, the believers made their first convert in Europe: Lydia, a dealer in purple cloth. She heard Paul preach and "she and her household were baptized" (16:15). Later proponents of infant baptism made much of this story, since they presumed that there would be infants somewhere in the extended family of her household. Here would have been a good time to make a point, if there were a point to be made, about excluding children from being baptized.

The story of Paul who, with another missionary named Silas, had been imprisoned at Philippi, reinforces this understanding of baptism. When an earthquake opened the prison, Paul and Silas did not seek to escape. An impressed jailer heard their message and asked, "What must I do to be saved?" (16:30). He was simply told that he should believe on the Lord Jesus, and then "you will be saved, you and your household" (16:31).

Those who hold to infant baptism are drawn to this story as well. On the down side for the cause of baptizers of infants, however, it can be said that the word *house* in the New Testament means too many things for anyone to argue conclusively that it implies the baptism of infants. At the same time, one cannot easily screen out anyone who usually would be considered a part of the household: servants, slaves, and, of course, children. It is important to recall that in that culture families were bonded in ways that we might not experience, living as we do in a time when nuclear families have split up or split from the territory, so people live far apart from their relatives. It was different in the time of the Ethiopian, Lydia, and the jailer. In the case of the jailer, in the middle of the night "he and his entire family were baptized without delay" (16:33).

At Corinth, a man named Crispus, an official of the synagogue, "became a believer in the Lord, together with all his household," and many other Corinthian hearers were also baptized (18:8). And in Ephesus, where Paul stayed to work longer than usual, he came across citizens who had not heard of the Holy Spirit, but had been baptized "into John's baptism." Paul told them that John, who had baptized with the baptism of repentance, told the people to believe the one who was to come after him—Jesus. "On hearing this, they were baptized in the name of the Lord" (19:5).

Finally, Paul provided a short biographical sketch in self-defense to an angry Hebrew crowd, reminding them of his time with Ananias, who had told him to "get up, be baptized, and have your sins washed away, calling on [Jesus'] name" (22:16).

Baptism in the letters of Paul

All of the gospel accounts were put down, set in order, edited, and made their appearance under the names Matthew, Mark, Luke, and John. The people who assembled the New Testament canon placed them first. In fact, however, the letters of Paul antedate them, and so words from the man whom Ananias baptized, and about whom the author of Luke-Acts reported, deserve examination as part of the original package of thought about baptism.

The first of these texts, Romans 6:3, is most decisive for the interpretation of baptism and for understanding the uses to which we are to put baptism daily and lifelong. The lines will reappear later in this book, but they deserve earliest mention:

> Do you not know that all of us who have been baptized into Christ Jesus were baptized into his death? Therefore we have been buried with him by baptism into death, so that, just as Christ was raised from the dead by the glory of the Father, so we too might walk in newness of life. (6:3-4)

Paul's letter to the Colossians has a parallel reference: "When you were buried with [Christ] in baptism, you were also raised with him through faith in the power of God, who raised him from the dead" (2:12).

Other Pauline references are also illuminating, but most are not as decisive. The important exception is a reference enriched by metaphor in Galatians 3:27: "As many of you as were baptized into Christ have clothed yourselves with Christ."

All the other references to baptism are in the first of two letters Paul wrote to a young congregation at Corinth, chiefly in the first chapter. While promoting the unity of the young Christian community, Paul showed how misinterpretations of baptism reinforced divisions among them. He was vehement in questioning the fighting factions, one of which, to his chagrin, identified itself with him. He asked, "Was Paul crucified for you? Or were you baptized in the name of Paul?" (1 Corinthians 1:13). He thanked God that he had baptized only two of them, so that, other than that pair, "no one can say that you were baptized in my name" (1:15). He went on to describe a division of labor; Christ did not send him to baptize, but to proclaim the gospel (1:17).

One hopes that in our own age of individualism, the baptized will regain a strong sense of community—a theme Paul stressed emphatically. He spoke of the believing community as being so intimate and so mutually committed that the metaphor of the body was appropriate in describing the community of the faithful:

> For just as the body is one and has many members, and all the members of the body, though many, are one body, so it is with Christ. For in the one Spirit we were all *baptized into one body*—Jews or Greeks, slaves or free—and we were all made to drink of one Spirit. (12:12, emphasis added)

While in some Christian traditions Jesus' emphasis on connecting baptism with "forgiveness" is stressed so strongly that it sometimes obscures other meanings, here the accent is on "unity," which is also emphasized in other communions and believed in by all. In the Pauline-style letter to the Ephesians, the bond of unity and communion is most profound, most urgently stated: "There is one body and one Spirit, . . . one Lord, one faith, one baptism, one God and Father of all" (4:4-5).

Also important and relevant for some of our later discussion is a text that appears in a late letter, 1 Peter 3:21, where the writer, talking about the flood in the time of Noah, mentioned almost casually that the water of that deluge prefigured baptism: "And baptism . . . now saves you—not as a removal of dirt from the body, but as an appeal to God for a good conscience, through the resurrection of Jesus Christ." In the flood, water destroyed, he argued, but now in baptism, water saves. When Christians argue about whether baptism symbolizes or effects salvation, that line of text is always cited and has to be taken seriously. Some scholars even believe that the whole first letter of Peter is a kind of instruction manual for those about to be baptized. One does not need to regard it as such a document, however, to be struck by the point that in the early church baptism was "saving."

What is baptism?

Having canvassed the New Testament references, we can suggest the following answers to that question as we seek to put baptism to use in our lives and in our time:

1. While baptism as metaphor can be by fire, cloud, or "in the Holy Spirit," in the practice of the church, *it always involves water*.
2. Baptism connects with the word of promise of the Father, who sends the Holy Spirit, and offers certain effects through baptism.
3. The effect most cited is forgiveness, which is related both to repentance and to being baptized.
4. The other frequently cited primal meaning focuses on unity, and thus community, on "one baptism," and on how all believers are made one through baptism.

If you are a seeker with a hungry heart, a burden of guilt, or the experience of disappointment, you will find that the New Testament commends the way of forgiveness, related to your baptism, as a prime resource for you. So far, at least, we have not heard of God withdrawing the promise of baptism, with its call to suffering—hence the danger—and to victory—thanks to identification with Christ "who was raised from the dead by the glory of the Father" so that we can "walk in newness of life."

4

———— ·◈· ————

The Useful Gifts
and Benefits of Baptism

WE NOTED THAT, from some angles, baptism is dangerous because it involves serious commitments and is misused harmfully when the baptized are casual or forgetful or slovenly about the sacrament and those commitments. Admittedly, very little in culture or church serves as a reminder of these dangers. It is easy to glide past the mentions of discipleship in the context of a worship service that includes baptisms amid the company of friends, soothing music, reassuring preaching, and prayers that address problems but can often come across as premature or superficial problem-solvers. Yet as Dietrich Bonhoeffer, the martyr to Hitler, reminded his readers in a book whose title in English became *The Cost of Discipleship,* following Jesus can be demanding and expensive.

Far short of the pain of physical suffering can be the creative agony of the baptized who experience doubt, temptation, or desert-dry spiritual life. If you have suffered any of these, you will recognize what the medieval scholars called *anomie*—the state of being incapable of responding to standards or norms for the good life—as well as *accidie*, which they called "the noonday devil." Thomas Aquinas described *accidie* as "sadness in the face of spiritual good."

The hope that baptismal promises will help us to thwart temptation, fertilize our spiritual life, and enable us to "get up" to enjoy spiritual good often seems unrealized—another illustration of the perils that come along with the benefits of baptism. The expectations and hopes that we are told to associate with baptism can get lowered or dashed among thoughtful baptized believers. They want to look ahead in faith, but find that baptismal commitments made long ago have grown dull. As a person of faith, you are to declare: "I am baptized!" But saying so does not always and immediately serve to fortify yourself. At such times there is reason almost to envy the religiously unstirred and uncommitted. The nonbelieving, the noncommitted do not have to waste a moment of prayer or reasoning when they ponder why their inner lives are so drab, their outlook so dim, their hope so wan. The baptized do not have such a sad luxury.

The cost of discipleship

The fact is, those promised gifts and benefits will not be realized or understood if the "cost of discipleship" is not mentioned. What, it is legitimate to ask, does an immersion do other than leave one gasping? Or what do three spoonfuls of poured water mean for the rest of life if one has not reckoned with the "alternatives" to the baptized life, to being "raised with Christ to newness of life"?

Here we must spell out clearly the baptismal address to these alternatives. The phrase "baptismal address" refers to that daily "return" to baptism that reaches as deep as John the Baptist's call to repent, to turn around, and is as inclusive as Paul's understanding that baptism affects *all of life,* including the believer's body, mind, soul, and context.

If there are hazards in baptismal faith, if there is a cost to discipleship, then those who are thoughtful, prayerful, and faithful about baptism and discipleship will have the assurance that the compensations of risk are rich. It is hard to picture someone who might face the sword, the fires, or the lions calculating a cost-analysis benefit. It is also difficult to picture a believer who takes the risks that could well lead to giving her life for another being busy with rational reckoning about those risks. Of course, that the hope of heaven has often been the unmentioned factor hardly needs mention here. Almost all the testimony of to-be-martyred believers has shown some faith in the promise of divine gifts in eternal life. But there is something greater, something deeper here. Countless Christians, believe it or not, do not make any magical "pie in the sky" something for which they bargain. *The love of God is all that is at stake.*

A tale I often cite (I am told it comes from the tradition of St. Bernard) shows what this higher-than-high reward is. In this story, a pilgrim has a vision in which he encounters a woman carrying a torch in one hand and a pitcher of water in the other. "Where are you going?" he asks. She answers: "I am going to use the water to quench the fires of hell, and the flame to burn the pleasures of heaven. *Then* people can start loving God for God's own sake."

Many people have shown—and people continue to show— such love in their witness, piety, writing, and action. The death of martyrs, like the deaths of everyone, forces them to face the abyss of mystery. Details of the life to come can be filled in with phrases from biblical texts or acts of imagination in music, art, and prayer—and yet the abyss remains. Heaven aside, the believer who takes the love of God seriously finds that acting in the presence and power of that love is its own reward—regardless of the risks.

Such examples are powerful if not overpowering. You may be thinking, "How could I possibly be thought of as a candidate to belong to a cast of such transcendently loving and beloved heroines and heroes?" But remember, the gifts and benefits of baptism are yours. Picture the gifts and benefits of baptism as the figurative elements in the bag or baggage you carry during life's pilgrimage—always there with you to be taken out and used. I am aware that in the Sermon on the Mount Jesus counsels disciples to travel light, and take no baggage, but I'll get off that hook by reminding you that this baggage is metaphoric, and only its contents are to be taken literally. I will now reach into thick texts and let them guide as our introductions to these "gifts and benefits."

Gifts and benefits of baptism

First, the fact that we baptize in the name of the Trinity, that is, "in the name of the Father and of the Son *and of the Holy Spirit*," has led countless commentators to stress that baptism opens one to the gifts of the Spirit. That such language is alive in our own time is apparent from ecumenical efforts to point to and detail the meaning of the Spirit in the many cultures that make up the global church.

In a notable and widely accepted document of the World Council Commission on Faith and Order, issued in Lima, Peru, in 1982, the drafters of *Baptism, Eucharist, and Ministry* had this to say in the section on "The Meaning of Baptism," where Section C is captioned "The Gift of the Spirit":

> The Holy Spirit is at work in the lives of people before, in and after their baptism. It is the same Spirit who revealed Jesus as the Son (Mark 1:10-11) and who empowered and united the disciples at Pentecost (Acts 2). God bestows upon all baptized persons the anointing and the promise of the Holy Spirit, marks them with a seal and implants in their hearts the first installment of their inheritance as sons and daughter of God. The Holy Spirit nurtures the life of faith in their hearts until the final deliverance when they will enter into its full possession, to the praise of the glory of God. (II Cor. 1:21-22; Eph. 1:13-14)

Even a genius with a quick ear and an accounting brain cannot take in all of that when hearing the words spoken during the brief minutes of a baptism. It takes about seven seconds to say, "(Name), I baptize you in the name of the Father and of the Son and of the Holy Spirit." Double that time in the case of infant baptism when it is interrupted by crying or by negotiation for position around the font by relatives who are holding and using cameras. The scene suggests that, for most people, every opportunity to ponder *the gift of the Spirit* has passed.

That being the case, I would suggest that you, as a Christian making the sign of the cross to token your own baptism, might reflect for a while on one of the above phrases for each of several mornings. Let me lift out some words you might well reflect on:

- *[The Spirit] is at work.* The affirmation that the Holy Spirit *is* at work in you is a reminder that baptism is not a mere ceremony designed to remind us that there are good stories in the New Testament about the baptism of Jesus and about "our kind" of baptism in the cases of an Ethiopian eunuch, a Macedonian seller of purple cloth and her family, or a jailer at Philippi and his family. Those stories are our benchmarks and earmarks, our inspirers and our judges. But they are of old. They happened; they are not now happening. I have long cherished the clumsy words of a European thinker who says that in worship, "something happens; it does not *not* happen." So in baptism, the Holy Spirit's work "is happening." Some scholars have pointed to the Holy Spirit as the one who assures us that God is present, and is not just a divine being from a distant past. So the first gift of the Spirit in baptism is the awareness that the Spirit is at work right now, the promised gift is being given now, in this baptismal moment and in the life of daily follow-ups. As a user of baptism you cannot lose if you daily reflect on the Spirit's presence in your life and in your world.

- *[The Spirit] empowered* the disciples, but in our understanding of the Spirit in the present tense, we can say that in baptism the Spirit *empowers* the adult or child who is being baptized. Here, as always, the dangerous side of baptism comes out with the gift. The power of the Spirit may someday lead the baptized one to have to speak inconvenient words to earthly powers in the name of Jesus. He might need to speak the truth when lies are the favorite content of discourse. She will need power to cling to faith when physical pain or temptation pulls her from it. In all such settings, the baptized

Christian has the right to call upon the empowering Spirit to get through a crisis, gain boldness to speak and act, and to enjoy the gifts.

- *[The Spirit] united* the disciples, and in our understanding of the Spirit at work also in the present we can say that in baptism the Spirit unites the baptized one with the family, congregation, communion, and whole Christian church that is involved with the baptism. The enduring appeal of unity is stronger than ever in a world and church where suspicion reigns more frequently than affirmation, where broken relations crowd out enjoyments of friendship, where derision and hatred mark factionalized congregations, and where the faith is sometimes used to promote violence. While the fullness of unity cannot be attained in earthly life, it becomes possible to revisit its promise, command, and process when a person recalls and affirms the unitive power of "one baptism."

- *[God] bestows . . . the anointing of the Holy Spirit.* The promise is that the Spirit will be poured out on *all* the baptized persons, as the text reminds us. *Anointing* is not a widely used term in the current world. One hears pentecostal and charismatic Christians talking about it, and they do the rest of the church the favor of demonstrating that the ancient gifts are not merely ancient. Another use of "anointing" occurs in many Christian rites when a person is near death. In these "last rites" he is symbolically being prepared for the fulfilled life with God. Third, and again in some Christian traditions, priests and bishops are anointed when they are ordained. Sadly, some televangelists peddle anointing oils and promise that they will produce miracles for those who pay for them and use them. For the rest, anointing is in a way figurative, and one does not need to use oils. What is striking in connection with baptism, as this document has it, is that *all* baptized persons are anointed, set aside, without distinction, to go about their work and mission.

- *[God] bestows . . . the promise of the Holy Spirit.* The concept of God's showering us is easier to grasp, thanks to the liveliness and memorability of the biblical stories in which the resurrected Jesus speaks of the Holy Spirit both as Promise and as promised. The gospels picture the Spirit not as a simple replacement of the bodily Jesus, who had been among them before and after the resurrection, but as the one who is present, who makes the risen Lord present. *Promise* is a rich word here. It comes from the Latin *"pro+missio"* and implies that something or someone is sent forth to do something. In Christian language, promise involves both having and hoping, realizing and expecting. The user of baptism who prays repentantly and returns to baptism daily is asking that this promise and sending forth be hers that day.

- *The Holy Spirit marks [all baptized persons] with a seal.* Through the ages the "sealing" with the sign of the cross—often with oil on the forehead of the baptized—has made this a rich experience for observers and can and should be a daily occasion for revisiting what the seal first meant. Some church traditions have let this experience of sealing fall into neglect and be forgotten, but in an era when sight and touch need to be ministered to, the physical marks of sealing, while they do not have any miraculous effects, signify the presence of grace which, come to think of it, *is* a miraculous effect. When you make (or "think") the sign of the cross, picture the meaning of this seal upon you, not visible on your body but visible and effectual *in your way of life.*

- *The Holy Spirit . . . implants in their hearts the first installment of their inheritance as sons and daughters of God.* Now the drafters of the document are really talking our language, since so many of us live in cultures where installment buying and selling make access to more products and experiences available that otherwise would not have been. It has to be noted that such installment buying can also bring burdens and lead to failures in ordinary life. In the extraordinary life of the Spirit, however, this first installment is part of a secure and enabling contract in which the life and death and resurrection of Jesus are the fulfillments in view, promised, and already partly realized. When you return in repentance and resolve to live your baptism each day, you are *not paying* one installment, but you are accepting what is already paid for as another installment of God's activity in Christ.
- *The Holy Spirit nurtures* the life of faith in the hearts of the baptized. It is hard to overstress this concept and the reality of nurture. The ongoing nurturing of the life of faith by the Holy Spirit counters the notion that because the *act* of being baptized is brief, unrepeated, and unrepeatable, it soon belongs to a person's past. The life of faith is nurtured and fed by other gifts of God as well, including the Lord's Supper, the hearing

of the Word, and carrying on the works of justice and mercy that derive from God.

A second example of some of the gifts and benefits of baptism can be found in the "Outline of the Faith" in the Episcopal Church's *Book of Common Prayer,* which strikes another note. Here the language of "grace" dominates as the theme of baptismal gifts.

Q. What is the inward and spiritual grace in Baptism?

A. The inward and spiritual grace in Baptism is union with Christ in his death and resurrection, birth into God's family the Church, forgiveness of sins, and new life in the Holy Spirit. (PBH, 858)

Each Christian tradition tends to draw a set of basic motifs from its reading of the gospel and its understanding of the Sacraments of Baptism and the Lord's Supper. Musicians speak of a *cantus firmus,* which gives support to and sustains all those delicate melodic lines above it. So the concept of "inward and spiritual grace" is the *cantus firmus,* the place where the Anglican Communion and the Episcopal Church within it come down. That does not mean that Episcopalians can claim a monopoly on the discourse about grace and these graces. They have the grace *not* to claim that. However, they do not want that keynote or accent to fade, and they do want to have it heard and realized among the baptized.

Now the accent is on *union* with Christ, which is another gift of baptism and the Lord's Supper. The sacramental community is not a burial society, a memorial association, an alumni group that looks back to the disciples. The union with Christ in baptism means that the baptized are as close to and as "knitted into" the fabric of Christ's life or, to change the picture, are made as much a part of the blood stream and pulse of his body as were the first baptized disciples.

Similarly, says the Episcopal Catechism, the baptized person experiences "birth into God's family, the Church." Most communions stress that, when possible, baptisms should occur in the context of the worshiping congregation (though intimate, familial, private baptisms also are effective) because it advances the realization that baptism is an incorporation, a becoming a part of the body of Christ which is the church.

Ours is a time of hyper-individualism in which many Christians feel they have to be "spiritual" on their own. Then they believe that they can serve as experts who are equipped to point to the flaws of the gathered body. In the face of that, it is vital to promote classic and biblical understandings of baptism. They are communal and corporate. They focus on bringing the baptized into a larger family than the biological one.

Next, the Episcopal Catechism stresses that a gift or benefit of baptism is "the forgiveness of sins," the gift that no one who wants to be faithful to the original commands and promises that we read in the biblical texts dare overlook. A believer who stresses the forgiveness of sins is not being a biblical literalist since the whole thrust of the gospel emphasizes this theme. We shall postpone elaboration for a moment.

The final "inward and spiritual grace in baptism" is "new life in the Holy Spirit." That stress is congruent with everything we said about repentance, which includes both presenting one's "old self" for baptism and the daily return to baptism through repentance and the receipt of grace. This return includes the expectation in faith and hope that the old will be done away with.

Having deferred stress on *forgiveness* for a moment, we now arrive at that moment, that basic motif, that *cantus firmus* in the

Small Catechism of Martin Luther, the most used instruction manual in healthy Lutheranism. Millions of children and other confirmands in this global community have memorized these lines:

> What gifts or benefits does baptism grant?
>
> Answer: It brings about forgiveness of sins, redeems from death and the devil, and gives eternal salvation to all who believe it, as the words and promise of God declare. (LSC, 46)

To some schools of Christianity, that short answer is a very offensive, almost scandalous passage, for a simple reason: they do not believe that baptism "brings about" anything, but is only a marvelous response on the part of believers to what God has done and a visible symbol of their act of faith. Since I am not going to spend pages revisiting centuries-old debates whose residue fills libraries on this subject, I beg your forgiveness.

I will disappoint you by stressing only the positive features in this understanding: baptism effects, it "brings about," forgiveness of sins. The author of the Catechism, Martin Luther, cites one biblical text that does not directly address this. Having said that "the Word and promise of God declare[s] these benefits," he goes on:

> What are these words and promises of God?
>
> Answer: Where our Lord Jesus Christ says in Mark 16:16, "The one who believes and is baptized will be saved; but the one who does not believe will be condemned." (LSC, 47)

Of course, forgiveness and salvation go hand in hand.

In the next part of his little chapter on baptism, Luther quotes St. Paul in Titus 3:5-8. That text says that "through the water of rebirth and renewal by the Holy Spirit" God "saved us." Some later commentators on the Catechism also made reference to a very late New Testament writing, 1 Peter 3:21: "And baptism . . . now saves you . . . an appeal to God. . . ." Luther sees all the "gifts or benefits" of baptism as components in the context of being "saved." Some are so important that they merit extended treatment, which he provided and we shall now bring up for reflection.

Baptism is useful in repentance and forgiveness

From page one we have connected baptism with both "danger" and "benefits." Seldom will the need for linking these two be more apparent than when we discuss their roles in the forgiveness of sins. Seldom will we find more difficulty than when we consider why the forgiveness of sins could ever be conceived of or experienced as dangerous. This is due to the fact that it is easy to dull the drama of forgiveness, living as we do in a culture in which divine forgiveness comes cheaply.

"Cheap grace" is a huge and risky reference, one that is hardly fair to all circumstances. Pastors, psychologists, family members, and friends are all aware of the situation of people who take sins and sinning very seriously. They also experience a profound need for being forgiven and feeling forgiven. Or, conversely, they know of people who were once burdened by sin but who now are and feel released, freed, and open to all kinds of futures.

Nevertheless, cultural analysts and our own eyes tell us that the concept of sin is often treated quite casually or even rejected. Certainly many in the public demonstrate that they hunger to hear gossip or actual charges against celebrities and people of public importance. When the stars fail, the paparazzi are there with cameras and the biographers with their laptops so they can publicize debasing and incriminating photos or salacious stories. Buyers of sensationalist magazines at supermarket check-out lines, or those who are addicted to watching trash-channels on television, or buyers of best-selling biographies can gain a magnified if distorted sense of their own virtue when they contrast their glories to the vices of "those sinners" out there. They know that those sinners will sooner or later say, as many today do, that "mistakes were made" and that God forgave them, so "let's get on with our lives." Similarly, when people of power fall, it provides a sense of superiority to their constituencies, be they employees, shareholders, students, or voters. You can hear the sneers: "They think they are so big, and here I catch them doing things you would never catch me doing."

Beyond such circumstances, the topics of sin and forgiveness are not very popular, and at baptism time this unpopularity is often on display. Autobiographical writings from people who have given up on the church or who triumphantly stamped out of it, as often as not, engage in blaming the church for harping on human frailty and failure. Some who have left the church claim they heard too many fire-and-brimstone sermons of the sort old-style evangelists used to favor. Life is hard enough, one will hear, without our having to learn that the world around us and the world of which we are a part are held to unreasonable standards of conduct. Why go to church and hear more? Such preaching, we are told, tends to make hypocrites of those who do show up to hear that there is a gap between what God expects and what we do.

Where talk of sin and forgiveness is not outright derided, it can also turn people away because they think that such talk is not realistic. Look around, we will hear, and you will find many people being good and doing good. The majority are not embezzlers, wife beaters, child abusers, or sexual scandalizers. Most people go about living relatively quiet lives, making a living, raising a family, having innocent good times. Why should they have to think in terms of sin and forgiveness, of the need for baptism and the gifts that come with it?

It has been said that there is nothing as useless as an answer to an unasked question. When people ask, "What must I do to be saved?" the church stands ready with good biblical answers. When people don't ask, however, or when they reject biblically based answers, it is perhaps because they think that there is something wrong with the diagnosis of human nature and action as sinful—as promoted by the church. As for the little or medium-sized sins that ordinary people commit, why make such a big deal of them? God is a forgiver who likes to forgive, so God will forgive petty offenses without much fuss. Why list sin and sins as something so important that baptism is needed to work against them?

Moderns get troubled when they hear the phrase "original sin," a term that often gets associated with baptism. That Christian expression is *not* in the vocabulary of Judaism, even though the Hebrew scriptures (the Old Testament of the Christian Bible) contain the story of Adam and Eve and the curse that came upon them when they were disobedient. Using this story, later Christians developed the notion of original sin with elaborate and often graphic descriptions of how the wrongdoing of Adam and Eve gets transferred through semen and bodily juices until "original sin" comes to be the second-most important thing to be said about the newborn, or about anyone else, for that matter.

Some traditions made matters even more shocking by speaking of "total depravity." *Depravity* is a word we normally reserve for particularly warped and weird bad people. Some Christians, however, have used that term with reference to a six-week old

Students of various cultures find that the baptized ranks include many who have such attitudes. Not too long ago, being baptized was simply a part of the legal culture in European states. Virtually every child was baptized unless parents made strenuous efforts to avoid baptism. If everyone "does it," or has "it," namely baptism, "done" to them as part and parcel of being born and getting a birth certificate, then the whole brunt of biblical teaching is lost. In such cases, the danger with baptism is that, apart from faith based on the Word of God that comes with the water of baptism, baptism can cheapen the human's relation to God and render blunt the sharp edges of divine demand and human response.

If Christians successfully sell short the meanings of sin, two issues remain: What does "forgiveness" mean, and why and how should we connect it with baptism? The scriptures are rich in stories, descriptions, and proclamations about forgiveness. In every case, being forgiven is the action of the Divine Lover who wills that the beloved become unburdened, free, ready for merciful action, and beautiful. Being forgiven is to have the weight lifted, the chains broken, the stigma erased, the charter for new life given.

Suppose we get this far in rephrasing biblical concerns; there is one more that is both meaningful and urgent in the present context. We have said that "baptism brings with it the forgiveness of sins." To aver something like that is to invite the charge from skeptics that, when baptism is not merely routine, it is seen to be almost magical. Pour some water on someone's head just once, and you create the impression that you have written a moral blank check to be filled out by every recipient. In a way, you have done this, though that way is different than the magic-minded believers expect. And Christians who baptize infants, but do not get this accent right, do invite legitimate criticism from sensitive and discerning souls who have a right to be offended. Can *this* be the kind of thing that in the gospel stories Jesus is pictured as having in mind when he commanded that his disciples baptize all nations?

Baptismal forgiveness does not say forgiveness is cheap but that it is both free *and* expensive. The baptized person is to *walk* in "newness of life," something that is very hard to do. His neighbors have sized him up and are ready with condemnations of the sinner. Then that sinner comes home from the church's font or the river, having gotten wet. That is to change everything? Well, actually it does—forgiveness is freely given and faith responds.

To keep things expensive, Christians remind themselves, as everyone's catechisms tell them, that baptismal water doesn't "do" anything on its own. In biblical writings, what matters is water that is associated not with magic but with faith, not human conjuring but divine blessing, and therefore the Word of God associated with this sacrament. *Baptism* is a word of promise and release. And faith is a *response* to the promise and the experience of being forgiven, committed, and challenged. Take away the word of promise or the faith connected with it and there is no chance that forgiveness will be offered.

For an adult or a child, while baptism is a once-for-always event, it is never a finished product. The thoughtful Christian who is ready to receive and use the full set of baptismal gifts "returns" daily and in various circumstances to her baptism. Pronouncing and receiving the forgiveness of sins now become stamped in memory and, as it were, on a body. If you ever feel haunted by guilt and sin after repentance and your return to the meanings of baptism, you are having trouble with believing the promises of God. If you put the word and promise of baptism to use, you will experience the forgiveness of sins and will be free to move among your fellows with an unburdened heart in newness of life.

Baptism redeems from death and the devil

The gifts and benefits of baptism include deliverance. A traditional catechism phrase that says baptism "redeems from death and the devil" sounds so shocking, so out of touch with reality, so ready to claim too much for the goods and benefits of baptism, that it could lead a thoughtful baptized person to be frustrated or envious. First, frustrated, because it is hard to get into one's head that baptism "redeems" from death. Envious, because while others seem or claim to be getting the point and the effects, I—a baptized person—am still aware of death and scared to death. And further, I am not sure that being free of "the devil" is my experience. After the daily return to baptism, do I feel delivered from any evil person or force or principle—a.k.a. the devil? And if I do think of myself as rescued, then why do I still have so many problems with myself, my neighbor, or my God?

If you are going to a baptism soon, observe closely. You are likely to find that the most embarrassing part of a baptismal liturgy in most churches is the moment when the baptizer asks the adult being baptized, or the godparents and parents of a child, something like, "Do you renounce all the forces of evil, the devil, and all his empty promises?" You are then going to hear parents, godparents, and *the congregation* answer, "I do."

Five hundred years after Martin Luther wrote a Q. and A. like that, Lutherans and their spiritual kin have still not found a way to get rid of those unfashionable lines about an invisible and unwelcome guest who is to be shooed away from the rite. Thus in *Evangelical Lutheran Worship* the direction appears:

> *The presiding minister addresses candidates for baptism as well as the parents and sponsors of young children. The assembly may join in the responses.*

Then the presider speaks to those present around the font:

> *I ask you to profess your faith in Christ Jesus, reject sin,*
> *and confess the faith of the church.*

Who would not be ready for such a direction? Why present one's self or someone else for baptism into the Christian faith and church if he is unready to profess faith in Christ Jesus? The almost-smuggled-in two little words, *reject sin,* sound innocuous enough; they slide right past the brain cells that pick up everything else. Yet we are not rid of the negatives; the presider continues:

> *Do you renounce the devil and all the forces that defy*
> *God?*
>   *Do you renounce the powers of this world that rebel*
> *against God?*
>   *Do you renounce the ways of sin that draw you from*
> *God?*

And in all three cases, the responses are:

> *I renounce them.* (LSC, 229)

It is a good bet that if one polled a confessing congregation, 99 percent or more of the members would have no trouble saying they renounce the ways of sin. In one way or another we think or say it every morning upon arising, or whenever we are faced with temptation and challenge. "Good-bye sin, good riddance! I sincerely intend to walk in the ways of God and to keep sin at a distance, or see it abolished in me, once again." By now "the ways of sin" are so familiar that we may almost regard them as old friends who are hardly threatening. They are within us, part of our secrets, elements of life that give us comfort, spiritual easy chairs to sink into, bad habits that come easily. Do we recognize "the ways of sin," the paths it takes, the manners it assumes, the masks it wears? Yes. The believer is given grace to renounce those ways and seek God's guidance for other ways.

The middle of the three terms in this part of a baptismal service also need not slow us down, though it might serve as an occasion for looking around at the world. It is the question about renouncing the powers of this world that rebel against God. Now, not to be bombarded with clues as to the powers of this world that rebel against God you would have to be deaf and blind, oblivious to signals from the mass media, beguiling friends, merchants of tempting products, and the promises of many politicians. These can all represent "the powers of this world." You hear about them in many a sermon or come across them when examining the interior of your heart. The resurrection of Jesus Christ was the decisive victory over the rebelling and negative powers of the world, but they still live on to tempt and plague all believers, life-long. Renounce them? "Glad to," the assembly members think. You can renounce them without embarrassment. Nonchurched friends and members of the community who are present to look on and support the baptized person or party can hear all this and not even feel the need to inquire about what it means.

Turn now to that first of the three questions, the one that sounds like an antique or quaint relic from biblical times or an age of superstition. Speaking of the devil and all the forces that defy God evokes images from an era when witchcraft and witch hunts were common. At the very least, mentioning the devil will call to mind pages of badly conceived cartoons of the devil as an impish, cunning, drooling character in a red union suit holding a trident in his hand.

The devil has not disappeared from pop culture, in which films like *The Exorcist* appeal to modern imaginations by suggesting that there are weird and threatening undertones and counterforces in our ordinary world. In entertainment, the devil exists to be taken seriously. In serious life, the devil is at best an entertaining, cartoonish figure. It is time to leave him and return to the scene of Christian liturgy.

Sometimes when you attend a service of worship in which someone is to be baptized, you will hear these words almost whispered, or they are read so rapidly that one might miss the words. Yet there they are. Here is the *Book of Common Prayer* of the Episcopal Church, a church body not usually known as one whose worship is designed to shock.

> *Do you renounce Satan and all the spiritual forces of wickedness that rebel against God?*
>> *Do you renounce the evil powers of this world which corrupt and destroy the creatures of God?*
>> *Do you renounce all sinful desires that draw you from the love of God?*

And, of course, three times the response comes in the words:

> *I renounce them.* (PBH, 302)

As before, the devil as an uninvited party-crasher who is about to be bounced is still on the scene, this time bearing the alternative name "Satan."

You may think we are making too much of this demonic character by reprinting lines from three different orders of baptism, but the repetition is calculated, designed for effect. To make way for confession of faith in Christ it is necessary to do some housecleaning or heart-cleansing, to wipe the cupboard bare of false gods, to force away the major antagonists of the baptized believer.

What is going on here is a vestigial version of the once-vibrant ceremony of exorcism. Renouncing the devil is an old custom in baptismal rites, going back at least to Hippolytus and the *Apostolic Tradition* in the second century. Exorcism is not mentioned in the gospel versions of Jesus' command to make disciples and to baptize all nations, but there is so much in the gospels' accounting of Jesus' ministry that is congruent with this line that to say, on baptismal day, "Begone, Satan!" or "Get thee behind me, Satan!" is perfectly fitting. The ancients made a profound and unforgettable point about this when they had the baptized person do this renunciation while shivering in the river or pool or at the font.

Hippolytus displayed a dramatic sense from which we might learn today: he wanted the candidates for baptism to face west during this portion of the service, to show that they were aware that as the sun goes down, so does the power of the devil. And in Eastern Orthodoxy, in many rites, the adult being baptized spits toward the west. In the case of infant baptism, it would be easy for the parent or godparent to turn so that the child faces west. (Most little babies do not need directions or prompting to spit, westward or not!)

Commentators often remark that Lutheran, Episcopal, and Roman Catholic liturgists have to work hard to keep these lines of renunciation in the service books, or to encourage their use in such books. In the explanation of the meanings and use of baptism, which we are using as background here, we read that just as baptism "brings about forgiveness of sins," so here it "redeems from death and the devil." That little half line still shocks some Christians, who see baptism as a mere symbol, an image of what has *already* happened in the life of the person being baptized. (Here we are talking about adult "believer's baptism.") She has heard the Word and brings her faith to the rite. She *has been* redeemed from death and the devil, and the ceremony itself is a vivid picture of that, a seal of what has happened.

Because of all the potentials for misunderstanding that can appear when Christians mention it, witness to the power of the devil in our time may, or perhaps should make, serious worshipers squirm. In a culture in which believers caught in a crime or under suspicion for shady activities try to get themselves off the hook by assigning blame—"the devil made me do it!"—it is wise and proper to be restrained about evoking any sense of satanic power.

I confess that when writing a short life of *Martin Luther,* I had difficulty dealing with the place of the devil in his thought. It was so tempting to turn Luther into a modern person by playing down "the forces of evil," somehow personified in an invisible figure, the devil. I was writing, however, in the shadow and under the influence of Heiko A. Oberman, as significant a Luther scholar as my generation had seen. Certainly that sophisticated scholar could have hidden the devil behind the scenes or between the lines or inside the index of his book. Instead he titled his most influential work *Luther: Man Between God and the Devil.*

Oberman, contributing to my uneasiness, dug up all kinds of things a twenty-first century heir of this tradition might like to forget. When in 1533, Luther remembered his childhood home, he did not depart from its ethos when he showed that he believed it to have been hovered over and afflicted by witches. Oberman argues that "Luther's world of thought is wholly distorted and apologetically misconstrued if his conception of the Devil is dismissed as a medieval phenomenon and only his faith in Christ retained as relevant or as the only decisive factor."

In fact—and I wished this were not true—Oberman says that Luther did not merely inherit a medieval sense of the presence and power of the devil: he enlarged and intensified it. Here is the sentence from which Oberman got his title: "There is no way to grasp Luther's milieu of experience and faith unless one has an acute sense of his view of Christian existence between God and the Devil. Without a recognition of Satan's power, belief in Christ is reduced to an idea about Christ—and Luther's faith becomes a confused delusion in keeping with the tenor of his time" (104).

Oberman saved the day when he showed that, while the entire Reformation, Protestant and Catholic, kept a focus on the devil, "Luther distinguished sharply between faith and superstition." So by writing about the devil he was also engaging in exorcism, a driving out of Satan: "Unlike any theologian before or after him, [he] was able to disperse the fog of witches' sabbath and sorcery and show the adversary for what he really was: violent toward God, man, and the world." This detour into a biography of Martin Luther is intended to help lead us to the key point: "to make light of the Devil is to distort faith. 'The only way to drive away the Devil is through faith in Christ, by saying: "*I have been baptized, I am a Christian.*"'" (p. 105, Emphasis mine)

Luther could seem to reflect medieval superstition when he reported that in the monastery he heard sounds that he attributed to the devil. Yet this devil was not a poltergeist but the adversary of the Word of God. So he added calmly, "But when I realized that it was Satan, I rolled over and went back to sleep again." The ability to come to such repose is a free gift of faith received in the context of a repentant and faithful life, a life within which one can say "I am baptized" and know that it means I am "redeemed from death and the devil." Our concern for the daily return to baptism, shown in the suggestion that one should start and end the day with the sign of the cross as a token of baptism, is warranted by the constant freedom of the baptized to exorcise evil powers—not just on the day of baptism but through all of life.

Baptism gives eternal salvation to all who believe it

Baptism is not only about something that happens on the day of baptism, nor is it useful in daily practice only until physical death. According to the baptismal service, baptism brings with it the gift of eternal life "to all who believe it." That phrase, "to all who believe it," belongs with the two earlier claims as well: baptism "brings about a forgiveness of sins . . . to all who believe it" and "it redeems from death and the devil . . . all who believe it." I repeat that phrase to stress that the tie between baptism and belief is central in all that baptism is and does.

We reflect on the verb: baptism "gives" eternal salvation. The minister of baptism makes the sign of the cross and adds that the baptized person is "sealed by the Holy Spirit" and "marked with the cross of Christ forever." Of course, you as a believer affirm that this baptismal mark lasts lifelong, through the three or four score years given so many humans. But you now hear that the mark of God's promise is fulfilled because it lasts "forever."

When the artists created stained-glass windows or mosaics for medieval cathedrals, they portrayed Christ in glory, picturing him crowned and robed as a splendid monarch. But the images also show that glorious Christ still bearing wounds from the nails of the cross on his palms and the mark of the spear in his side. In the biblical testimonies that adore Christ as "highly exalted" and as having been given a name above every name, he bears the marks of his suffering and shame, but he is now glorified "forever."

So it is with the marks of your baptism. Baptism "gives" eternal salvation to all who believe it. This baptism is not just an item in an old story, a reminiscence of Jesus. It is not just a sign that we have converted and come to faith, that we are on the path to eternal life and salvation. Instead, here and now—baptized readers might check their files or the framed certificate on the wall to date the event—and from that date on, the believer has a warrant, a guarantee, a realized gift of "eternal salvation," which has already begun.

As hard as it is to imagine or picture the forces of evil, now we are asked to envision something more challenging, more difficult, but more promising: eternal life. If the devil is often reduced to a cartoon character, so the envisioning of eternal life also often takes on the appearance of caricatures. At once the following symbols come to mind: clouds, bearded and robed gatekeepers, one of them (probably St. Peter) keeping an account in the books, golden gates, harps, and other boring signs and symbols. Boredom. Eternal life does not sound very promising to a squirming boy who cannot tolerate a long rainy Sunday afternoon. To baptize someone for such an existence does not seem to be much of a gift.

A clue to the drama of what it means to be given eternal life appears in discourses of Jesus in John's gospel. There it is clear: *where he is and where there is belief, eternal life has already begun.* True, when believers gather for praise of God, they may make no distinction between the baptized and those who are welcomed guests, some of whom may be on the way to baptism. In the gospels, Jesus commands and commends all people to each other's care. They are to find Jesus, in the least of those who share life in the world with him (Matthew 25:31ff.).

At the same time, while the mark of baptism is invisible, the company of the baptized are visible when they recite the creed, attend the Lord's Table, read the scriptures, or use their own words to witness to the Word as they serve God in the world. In such ways, the baptized signal that eternal life has already begun for them. Here is a piece of good advice to fellow worshipers or those who attend meetings and are participants in Christian works of love: get used to each other. You belong to an eternal communion that has begun. And baptism "gives" this life to all who believe. According to Martin Luther, the scriptures are clear: receiving forgiveness, being redeemed from death and the devil, and being given eternal life all depend on belief that originates in and is checked by reference to "the Word and promises of God" that declare it. Everything that Luther says about the gifts and promises of baptism relates to his conviction that the effects of baptism reach into the life eternal. There is no expiration date on the benefits baptism gives.

Baptism is useful when one believes the promises of God

This can be a short section, since one does not need a long text to back up the assertions. This word and promise appear specifically in the Gospel of Mark:

> The one who believes and is baptized will be saved; but the one who does not believe will be condemned. (16:16)

If the forces of gravity could be collapsed into a black hole, scientists hypothesize that such a hole the size of a billiard ball would weigh as much as our whole world. Sometimes a short biblical verse carries such strength, force, and weight that it serves as a figurative black hole. It is all there, packed into the word *believes*, as in "one who believes and is baptized" or again in the word *saved*, as in "will be saved."

In the waters of baptism, connected with the Word and belief, one is "saved" by the visit of the divine Spirit who once "moved over the waters" as God created heaven and earth. The creed recited at baptism begins with the affirmation that God is the creator. We reaffirm that you, the baptized person, are fashioned along with all of creation, and are nourished and sustained along with all other living things. We are not talking about someone being saved simply because she is joined to the creation. Something happened that spoiled this creation. So, through the liturgy of baptism, the baptized person, or those representing her as an infant, receive a short course in being saved.

Thus, the order of baptism may include the words, "Noah and his family" were chosen and "saved." We may not be proud of Noah, the believer in God who did not argue with God to prevent the destruction of sinful humanity as Moses did when God would have destroyed the Hebrew people. Noah makes an unlikely hero of faith. Yet in the mystery of faith he is "chosen," and is prominent in the family of faith to which the baptized person is joined.

What is more, although most twenty-first century believers live far from Egypt and are not in any immediate sense members of the people of ancient Israel, we are members of the same family of faith and so, in many baptismal ceremonies, we affirm that by baptism we are saved by "being led . . . out of slavery into the freedom of the promised land," which can be anywhere and anytime. When the ceremony revisits the story of Jesus' own baptism, there is no word of *his* being saved because he is the Savior, but as we are identified with him in "the baptism of his own death and resurrection," we learn what being saved means for the baptized people of God: the beloved Son "has set us free from the bondage to sin and death, and has opened the way to the joy and freedom of everlasting life." Baptismal water is "a sign of the kingdom and of cleansing and rebirth," which are also parts of being saved.

Virtual oceans of ink have been spilled over the last ten words in Mark 16:16, which appear after the promise that those who believe and are baptized will be saved. They read, "but the one who does not believe will be condemned." Condemning here must mean being cut off from salvation, not being saved.

Many have drawn comfort from the fact that this remembered word of Jesus does not say, "but the one who is not baptized and does not believe will be condemned." If that negative phrase about not being baptized were in the text, Christian care would have developed differently. It would mean that every child who dies before being baptized, every catechumen preparing for baptism who suffers a fatal accident, every sailor who is not yet baptized but was converted aboard ship and later went down with his ship, would know no waters of salvation. Were not being baptized the cause of condemnation, the teachers of those preparing for baptism would have to hold crash courses and speak fast so that those being instructed could be quickly baptized and so not risk condemnation.

All such understandings make a desperate game out of what is essentially a word of promise. There is no such danger. Where infants are to be baptized, parents may safely wait some months until fathers finish a military tour of duty so they can be present for the event. For centuries, Catholics attempted to minimize the grief of the parents of deceased unbaptized babies by conceiving of a place or state called *limbo* where, through all eternity, such babies would not suffer, although they would be in an eventless place, there to be denied the vision of God. Small comfort that was to parents. The teaching about limbo, long fallen into neglect because it was so uncomforting and not supported in Scripture, is now replaced by new assertions about the encompassing love of God that embraces even the as yet unbaptized.

Given all the possibilities, church leaders increasingly con-
cluded that it is advisable in such cases to deal with the known,
not the unknown. Through the ages, as records show, heartless,
too-sure-of-themselves priests and pastors left parents of the
unbaptized in doubt and agony. Was their child "saved"? Such
fear, however, overlooks the fact that we are here dealing with "the
Word and promise of God." The Word and belief in the Word of
promise are what save and what bring all the gifts and benefits of
baptism. Today we proclaim a faith that is also as old as the scriptures, and most basic: God is a God of love who reaches out to
extend the covenant to ever more people. God "saved" the people
of Israel long before the baptism into Christ was announced and
before its explicit promises took effect.

Some elements in the Christian church long talked about the
"baptism of desire." Others stressed that in this text Jesus condemned not the failure to be baptized "on time," but the acts of
disdaining or rejecting baptism, or, in this case, despising baptismal faith.

All this talk about "Word" and "promise" may, for the
moment, seem to be a diversion or a distraction for the natural
question that follows: What is it about this water?

5

Water Alone Is Useless in Baptism

TALK ABOUT BAPTISM is dangerous because it can so easily be misinterpreted and can thus lead to chaos or be confused with magic or superstition. We have been finding so much meaning in the water of baptism that the unwary could get the impression that it "does" all the things claimed for baptism. So now we have to minimize the danger by putting up a figurative billboard-sized notice, and I quote: "Clearly the water does not do it," but (I am still quoting) what "does it" is "the Word of God, which is with and alongside the water, and faith, which trusts this Word of God in the water." The quote is from Luther's Small Catechism. Elaborating further, we read:

> For without the Word of God the water is plain water, and not a baptism, but with the Word of God it is a baptism,

that is, a grace-filled water of life and a "bath of the new birth in the Holy Spirit." (LSC, 47)

Plain water

It is hard to picture anyone thinking that "plain water" does anything that produces "the new birth" or brings the gifts and benefits of baptism. That "plain water" does beneficial things is not contested. Observation, common sense, and plenty of biblical stories suggest how useful and creative water is. While water— plain water—can threaten because it can cause drowning, water— plain water—is also the site of rescue. Non-swimmers who did not want to be in the water or those who suffer some misfortune that threatens them with drowning, but who are pulled out from water, recognize its power and, with it, the joy of their own lives that follows rescue.

Similarly, "plain water" is the main agent in washing, and thus deserves celebration as the chemical combination H_2O. Whether mixed with soap or not, it cleanses the body and other objects. One feels almost foolish reminding others of this basic lustrating function. Yet such reminding is in order because so many rites in many religions have been associated with washings that the biblical version that Christ commanded might occasion a celebration of water for its own sake, as rites in many religions do. Anyone who has come from a desert trek or a hot and brutal athletic combat relishes and wallows in the cool water of cleansing. Many who have had muscle or tendon injuries head for the warm baths, where "plain water" eases pain and promotes healing. We do not underestimate the values and many uses of "plain water." But it cannot do what the water of baptism does when it is connected with the Word of God.

Water and the Word

All commentators who try to explain why water, the visible element in baptism, gets associated with spiritual gifts and benefits have to wrestle with the means and meaning of this "connecting." Always it is the Word that matters, the Word that is essential for any sacramental benefits. In the case of Luther's Small Catechism, which is so helpful in providing a frame for all that we want to picture coming out of baptism, some prepositions come into play and we will now take note of them.

Sometimes when the sacrament is the Lord's Supper and the elements are bread and wine, we struggle with prepositions. Jesus Christ is truly present, we affirm, in connection with those elements, but how? We read that "in, with, and under" the bread and wine, which utterly retain their molecular structure, Christ's body and blood are present. So now with baptism, the Word of God is *with* and *alongside* the water. One line later: the Word of God is *in* the water. Whoever tries to explain the connection will soon have to withdraw and invoke mystery.

How the Word of God is *with* and *alongside* the water, or *in* the water is not visible to the eye or subject to chemical analysis. After a baptism where a basin or font is employed, the baptizers or their custodians routinely splash the water onto the ground and let it soak in. The mere elements are indeed "mere." So the whole focus is on the Word. A good question follows: if the Word does all this, why bother with water at all? Is it used to render a church ceremony more interesting, more memorable than one would be in which parents merely dedicated a child and only words are heard? Why use water at all in the case of adults who have not been previously baptized, but who now want to join the church? Why not just "sign them up," or why not invent a little ceremony for children in which, for instance, a church leader hands the godparents a rose, or says a prayer. Why not? Because water has to be the element, water has to be there.

Danger! We are back on the edge of reducing all this to magic or symbolism, something that is not allowed to happen in a biblically-based understanding. Again, it is as important to examine the Word of God in connection with baptism as it is unimportant to examine the molecular structure of water before, during, or after the rite. *"With the Word of God it is a baptism, that is, a grace-filled water of life."* This text does not say that the water plus the Word serve to remind us that God is good. It does not say that we are doing something that will make grandparents happy and proud. We are saying that water-plus-Word is "grace-filled."

We read that when Mary was blessed at the time she heard and accepted in faith that she was to become the mother of the Savior Jesus, the angel said to her, "Hail, Mary, full of grace." All believers who receive the divine gifts are properly spoken of as full of grace. Here a physical substance, water, is "grace-filled." The only way one can speak of that and be faithful to biblical concepts and promises of grace is to put the stress on the Word, which "fills" the water with grace, namely with saving power, which is unsought, undeserved, and free. And with the Word, the water is "a bath of new birth in the Holy Spirit." The person has experienced a first birth upon being born as a physical being. Now this birth is "new." Once again, water, "plain water," by itself cannot do what baptismal water "with the Word" can, namely to effect a new kind of birth, the one to which in baptism is renewed whenever you return, whenever you repent, whenever you thoughtfully make the sign of the cross as a signal that baptism has occurred and grace has been newly experienced.

The Word does it. When the Creator created, namely when the Spirit "moved on the waters" and chaos became cosmos, disorder became order, and a hopeless mess became a grand universe, the book of Genesis tells us, "Then God said. . . ." That phrase occurs many times in the first chapter of Genesis, on the first page of the scriptures, which are received as the Word of God. The shaping of the universe in this faith-full version does not contradict other poetic or scientific ways of speaking about the origin of the universe.

In the creation story as Jews and Christians receive it, God speaks and that speaking is the agency of creation itself. It is true that on occasion, including in the story of the creation of the human in the image of God, God appears as a sort of sculptor, a molder of clay, a doer with divine hands—hands that have never been any more visible to human eyes than are the eyes of the invisible God who "saw that it was good." For the rest, the Word of God is enough.

The Word was the agent of creation. Through the Word, God made a covenant with people, and through the Word, God blessed them. Through the Word, God led them to freedom. The Word commanded Noah to make an ark, a vessel that would save him and his family. The Word led Israel out of Egypt, and commanded the painting of doorposts with blood so Israel would be saved through a flight out of Egypt. Hundreds of times on the pages of the Bible we read that ours is a God who has spoken and who speaks now, in the command to baptize and in the promise that seals it. Now it is the Word that takes "plain water" and makes it "a bath of the new birth," whose agent is the Holy Spirit.

Once more, why not dispense with the element, meaning, why not throw out the water *before* receiving the infant or the adult into the community? Christians give several answers: they use water, with the Word, because Jesus commanded it. They use water, with the Word, because in the gospel words, Jesus offered promises with it. They use the Word alongside the water, because with the Word, the Spirit at the first birth of the universe is present now to effect the "new birth in the Holy Spirit."

Christians who respond to the command as they hear it in the Bible are quite precise about associating the Word "in" and "with" and "alongside" the water. They want to follow the command and accept the promise. The Word here is "in the name of the Father and of the Son and of the Holy Spirit." Some Pentecostal "Jesus-only" Christians baptize in the name of Jesus only, not invoking the Trinity. Some adapters who try to speak the language of the day, this day, this passing day, translate the names of the Trinity into words that they think better convey the intent of the words. Yet most Christians will baptize in the name of the divine Trinity, not as a magic incantation but as a faithful following of the divine command that connects baptism today with baptism for twenty centuries. The witness is to God as the creator of the baptized person and of the water used. God gives the command to baptize and seals the promise through the Son. The Holy Spirit, witnessed to in Genesis chapter one, is present and offers grace and new birth. The Word does it all.

In the New Testament, the Word refers as often to Jesus Christ as it does to any scriptures. He is the Word as the voice of God, the speaker of saving words. Secondarily, but not unimportantly, that term *Word* gets carried over and applied to the sacred scriptures. They are the record, agent, and carrier of the divine speech and action, without which one would not have seen God revealed in Jesus or in the Holy Spirit, the giver of new life.

Faith that trusts the Word in the water

Even referring to the Word alongside the water and calling it the agent of the new birth is not enough to complete the transaction of baptism. The text we are using is clear. What "does it," what gives the great benefits, is "faith, which trusts this Word of God in the water." The faith as described here is not an achievement, a sign that the baptized one is so good, so smart, so deserving, so comprehending that God has no choice but to hand out ribbons and trophies indicating victory to the person for gaining the new birth. Faith also is a gift of grace in which one grows.

The baptism of infants is an offensive or at least puzzling act to many because everyone knows that the baby does not "know" what is going on when the baptizer uses the words, and may "know" no more than to react with a shudder or a howl when water is applied. The child's baptism makes many glad. This includes all who are part of the Christian church, the body of Christ, the community of faith to which the child is now attached as an integral part and within which the child will "grow in faith, love, and obedience to the will of God." The baptism of a child brings joy to the local, intimate, familial, and congregational persons who are on the scene at this particular baptism. They are representatives of the millions, now billions, of the baptized who were and are the body of Christ before this new "new-born" joins them. We recall once more that the one who "*believes* and is baptized" is the one who is saved.

Biblical support for what faith, Word, and water do

All this language about what water connected with the Word "does" needs scriptural support, which can be found in Titus 3.

Speaking of the Word, this grace-filled water of life, and this "bath of the new birth in the Holy Spirit," the text tells us that we are saved

> through the water of rebirth and renewal by the Holy Spirit. This Spirit he poured out on us richly through Jesus Christ our Savior, so that, having been justified by his grace, we might become heirs according to the hope of eternal life. The saying is sure. (LSC, 47)

A footnote in *The New Oxford Annotated Bible* in the New Revised Standard Version offers a summary comment: "*The water of rebirth* combines two pictures descriptive of baptism: the washing away of sins (Acts 22.16; Eph 5.26), and rebirth, the beginning of a new life (Jn 3.5)" (313 NT). For anyone who may think that this single verse freezes the text about water and forces us to skate on thin ice, it is helpful to visit the three other New Testament verses listed in this footnote.

First, we go to Acts 22. In this story, which we looked at earlier, Paul reports on his encounter with "a certain Ananias, who was a devout man according to the law and well spoken of by all the Jews living there" (22:12). It was Ananias who came to the temporarily-blinded Paul and spoke the word through which he regained his sight (22:13). Then Ananias communicated God's call to Paul to be God's "witness to all the world" (22:15), and followed up with a question: "And now why do you delay? Get up, be baptized, and have your sins washed away, calling on his name" (22:16).

No mention is made of Paul's own faith, though it is clearly implied and reinforced in all the stories about Paul and in the letters he wrote. Here, simply, baptism—along with calling on Jesus Christ's name—washes away his sins.

A second and similar text is found in Ephesians 5:25-26: "Christ loved the church and gave himself up for her, in order to make her holy by cleansing her with the washing of water by the word."

And the third reference is the familiar discourse in John 3 between Jesus and Nicodemus, "a Pharisee" and "a leader of the Jews," who came to Jesus by night and asked about the signs Jesus was doing. Jesus responded by announcing that no one could see the kingdom of God "without being born from above" (3:3). The old King James Version and the New English Bible have it "born again," though most contemporary translations favor "born from above." Controversy over the preferred translation of the Greek term, depending as it does on context, need not slow us down here. The current point is that being "born from above" *or* "born again" is connected in the Gospel of John with water: "Jesus answered, 'Very truly, I tell you, no one can enter the kingdom of God without being born of water and Spirit'" (3:5).

As the footnote quoted above reminds us, the use of water with the Word was connected both to washing and rebirth. Baptism— water with the Word—accomplishes both according to both the New Testament and Christian tradition.

6

The Significance of Baptism
with Water

ONCE THE CONNECTION between Word and water is fixed in the consciousness of the Christian community and in the mind of each believer, a major question demands attention. It will throw more light on the concept of using baptism. In the Small Catechism Martin Luther asks, "What then is the significance of such a baptism with water?"

So far we have been discussing what water+Word+faith "do" through baptism. Now the language shifts from what they do to what baptism symbolizes, signs, or signifies. *Significance* refers to something that is not obvious, not readily visible, not easily noticed. It infers that there are meanings that do not strike a person if she is not being attentive, not ready to notice subtleties. We are being urged, "Stop! Let's go deeper" than the outward appearance of a ceremony and the presence of water suggest.

The sacrament makes use of symbols that are bound to the reality that is being celebrated and put to work. Thus water is not an arbitrary symbol. It would not do to substitute pomegranate juice or cola, since one does not wash in such liquids. Water, this most basic fluid, most abundant and practical for washing—and ominous because one can drown in it—is integrally tied to the meanings of baptism. Accept no substitutes! And yet, the believer is told to wonder about the significance, to look for more reality than the surface symbols or descriptive words of baptism signify. Again, from Luther's Small Catechism:

> Baptism with water signifies that the old person in us with all sins and evil desires is to be drowned and die through daily sorrow for sin and through repentance. (LSC, 48)

Where did this "old person" come in?

In certain traditions, seniors with long memories may recall a phrase in the Catechism that says that baptism with water signifies that "the Old Adam in us" should be drowned and die. The original languages of the passage agree. The German said that *der alte Adam*—in Latin, *vetus Adam*—is to be drowned. Modern translators evidently do not want to take readers down complex biblical bypaths when they can get the original's point across without confusion. They recognize that Adam appears because in Paul's letter to the Romans the "old person," who shows up in the modern translation we are discussing, is identified with the "one man" who, in the Genesis story of Adam, trespassed, thereby bringing sin and death into the world (Romans 5:12ff.). You are to see yourself as the "one man," who became "the old Adam" in the Catechism and in colloquial speech. Today in colloquial language some still blame "the old Adam" when they do wrong.

The death of your old person

The rich baptismal imagery here indicates that the "old person in us . . . is to be drowned and die." Sneaked into this phrase is one of the most important lines for anyone who wishes to make use of baptism, as every Christian will and must. This drowning, we read, occurs through "daily sorrow for sin and . . . repentance." We began this discussion of baptism by reference to "dailiness." You, the baptized Christian, are "born again," once and for all. But as you use baptism each day, you can look back and say you have been "born again, and again, and again." The death of which Paul speaks occurs with the dying of the old person, the old self, through "daily sorrow." Such sorrow does not mean that the baptized Christian is to develop into a morose, melancholy, mopey, and thus self-centered being. The kingdom of God is not served through superficial emotional contortions. Different people manifest differing patterns, so we do not look for one form of expression. Sorrow here goes much deeper than emotions. It involves bringing one's self before an awe-full God who does *not* act tyrannously, but who still holds the believer to account and who expects a moral reckoning. Such reckoning is intended to position the repentant person so he can accept grace and the removal of the list of sorrows from his slate. Repenting involves a complete 180-degree turn, a wiping of the slate clean, a saying good-bye not simply in mourning but basically with a push-away uttered as, "Begone!" "Out of my way!" "I'm on to you, now let me move on with a new life."

Repentance accompanies all this sorrowing and, in fact, the act of repenting is more assertive and aggressive than is the mere act of expressing sorrow daily. Repentance is not a grudging parting with the old ways and the old life. If the Word of God has reached the inner being enough to occasion repentance, the penitent person will have engaged in or have been led into a complete turning to God, to the new.

A new you and a new life before God

This talk about the death of the old person is not, however, the last word; it is followed by a more positive picture of what baptism signifies:

> and daily a new person is to come forth and rise up to live
> before God in righteousness and purity for ever. (LSC, 48)

This rising is what accompanies the use of baptism, that daily turning, especially in the morning prayer of the baptized who make the sign of the cross and know that it is somehow significant. The resurrection image that goes with these words of Paul is obvious, and is to have an impact on the life of all the baptized each day: "daily a new person is to come forth." The human body after baptism bears the same visible features as before, but hidden from view is the grace that takes the form of a new ability for you, the baptized, "to come forth and rise up." You come up from the river to walk through the paces and trials of a new day as a new person who gets to live "before God in righteousness and purity forever."

The appropriate question follows:

Where is this written? Answer:

> St. Paul says in Romans 6:3-4: "We have been buried
> with him by baptism into death, so that, just as Christ

was raised from the dead by the glory of the Father, we, too, might walk in newness of life." (LSC, 48)

The best way for St. Paul to make clear that the blessing of God and salvation from God are spontaneous is to associate them with baptism. Here is why: in this sacrament the human does not work to please God and does nothing to merit the notice or favor of God. Paul had just shown that he was aware of the dangers of this teaching: if forgiveness was free, why shouldn't we keep on sinning? So much grace is available! The apostle answered his own question: Should we sin more so that grace can overflow? "By no means!" (Romans 6:1ff.). The believer, through baptism and faith, is so closely bonded with Christ, so much a partner with Jesus in his suffering and death, and so immediately identified with the new life in Christ, that sin is out of place. This linking of you and Christ occurred in and with baptism.

"We have been united with him in a death like his" (Romans 6:5). Paul's word, quoted in the Catechism text, observes the new person emerging from baptism to live before God through grace and thus now able to live "in righteousness and purity forever."

Being buried with Christ

The symbolism of this identification is more dramatic, shocking, and therefore memorable, in Romans 6 than anywhere else. Once more, what happens in baptism? "We have been buried with him by baptism into death."

Those of us in the vast Christian majority that does not insist on immersing the whole body of the person being baptized have to interpret the significance of what we are doing. Those who preach and educate on the basis of Romans 6, which does not command any particular form of baptizing with water, should take time during baptismal instruction to tell stories about when and where and why some Christians baptized, or now baptize, by fully immersing the body of the one to be baptized. It is a powerful, visual symbol of being buried with Christ by baptism into death. The preacher might ask congregations and families to imagine the drama of the plunge into the mucky waters of rivers or the icy waters of cisterns. Then they might tell about the reception the ancient baptized converts received from people on the shore, or about the splendor of lamps that surrounded the just-baptized in a setting that as often as not occurred in near darkness. It was difficult in those days to miss the reality of having been "buried" with Christ by baptism.

In all sacramental acts something symbolic occurs that inspires interpretation. Thus in most observances of the Lord's Supper today there may be few remaining evidences of a supper being supped. Now and then Christian congregations will act to recreate something of the original setting for the meal, but they make clear that the central feature is always not a historic drama but the bread and wine that is blessed with the Word and taken with thanksgiving. So with this sacrament, those who believe that baptism by immersion is not the only commended and sanctioned form will responsibly apply water and then hear the language of Romans 6:4 applied and hopefully explained. They recognize that the effect does not depend upon the modes and amounts of water used. What matters is that there be some measure of water, and that it is always to be connected with God's word spoken and enacted in the context of belief.

Being raised with Christ

Next, "just as" Christ was raised from the dead by the glory of the Father, you, the baptized, long before your death and apart from Christ's return in glory, have already been "raised." It happened when you came up from or away from baptism, which was the event of your identification with the risen Christ. This is not at all the same as saying you have come forth "more or less as" Christ was raised. Once more, it is "just as. . . ." This rising enables you to walk in newness of life. In infant baptism, as the child develops and begins to walk, and also to walk in faith, she gets to walk "just as" Christ walked in his resurrected life. When a very aged arthritic person is helped out of a wheelchair and supported with canes so she can walk, her walking is still "just as Christ" walked, namely, in the "newness of life"—that is, in righteousness and purity before God. It is "in order to walk in newness of life" that so many Christians begin their day's walk by re-identifying themselves with Christ at baptism.

7

The Dangers and Rewards
of Infant Baptism

CONTRASTING THE WALK in newness of life by a very old person with the crawl of a baby prompts us to give attention to the most taken-for-granted feature of baptismal practice by the Christian majority and the feature most debated by large Christian minorities, namely infant baptism. If today's believers wish to understand and appreciate the grace that comes with this washing and wish to use their baptism, they need to recognize the risk and danger to their well-being—and to the well-being of a baptized child—if baptism's meaning is neglected and baptismal commitments are forgotten.

We revisit the scene of an infant baptism

Uncles who seldom wear neckties to church are wearing them today, and little cousins will be crowding around the font if adults will let them. These children may be hushed or they may out-squeal the baby who is being baptized. The aunts will be there in their finery. The oven-timers back at home are set so the roast will not be burnt. Cameras are poised, sometimes to the point that they distract from the sacramental event itself. The church floor feels secure, the entry doors are quietly being observed by welcoming ushers. Everything about the event suggests safety or security. There will be smiles on the faces of adults who, if they thought about what they are seeing, might be quickened from reverie to ask, "What are we doing here?" "What's going on?" "Whatever possessed us to make such a commitment and voice these words for our child?" All are good questions that might arise when someone wearing a robe reads some scripture, asks some questions, and pours water on the head of a cross-marked baby.

The commitment that accompanies and follows the reception of grace in baptism is to be grasped as something that puts the baptized on a perilous and yet utterly rewarding course. Baptism can be dangerous for a number of reasons, beginning with the fact that the sacrament is offensive to God when people take it for granted. It will be a peril for unthinking parents and caregivers who are just having baptism "done." It is dangerous in cultures such as those in Catholic and Protestant Europe where, until a generation or three ago, virtually everyone was baptized in infancy. A baptismal certificate and registry at the church and civil offices was then taken for granted as a birth certificate and hardly less valuable as an identifier. And when the phrase "taken for granted" characterizes the ethos of a culture or a family, it is not likely that the people involved with the baptism will understand what it means.

Baptism is dangerous for those who, as parents or sponsors or godparents, pledge themselves to share in the spiritual nurture of the child, to pray for her, and when occasion allows for it, to teach her the ways of faith. We cannot judge hearts, and we should not prejudge the hearts of parents or of sponsors who make themselves available as godparents. Yet interviews with the members of any congregation will turn up what baptizing pastors all too often observe: many see baptism on the baptismal day as a "done deal." When an infant's dress or suit is later stored along with a certificate, napkin, and a candle, also stored and thus forgotten are all the pledges made to help the child both receive all the benefits of the baptismal promises and learn to walk in ways initiated by baptism.

Deadly indifference

It is clear that taken-for-grantedness and indifference, the normal enemies of the spiritual life, are abnormally deadening in the case of baptism and can contribute to spiritual death. Of course, neglected baptism is not the only agent or signal of such a descent toward spiritual death. Being regularly absent from occasions where the gospel is preached or taught and being distanced from the company of the fellow-baptized, who gather to support each other in faith, also lead to a deterioration of spiritual health. One might also mention failing to show up at the banquet that is the Lord's Supper and letting one's prayer life wane as still other ways that lead to deadly indifference and thus spiritual death.

Those, however, who receive, understand, welcome, and put to use their baptism by returning to it daily in the midst of often attractive perils receive a wakeup call that quickens their senses and opens their minds to the gifts of newness that God brings each day.

The danger of arguing about baptism

The baptism of infants can also be dangerously misused when it is reduced to a topic of argument instead of celebrated as a gift to be received. Rather than revisit all the controversies among Christians in conflict over baptism through the centuries, we will discuss only issues that relate to New Testament stories and descriptions. While we will pick up some clues that will dull the sharpness of the next few lines, let them first stand in bracing splendor. First:

> List all the arguments or narratives in the New Testament that clearly make the point of commanding baptism of infants.

There is nothing to write here. There are no such texts. Next:

> List all the arguments or narratives in the New Testament that clearly make the point of forbidding baptism of infants.

Again, there is nothing to write. There are no such texts.

> If the texts are not absolutely clear and determinative, why pay attention to them?

Answer: because what is at stake in these discussions can throw light on baptismal practices, and these can have a bearing on the heart of the Christian faith as understood in different communions.

We have finally only one interest, which is to bring forth what is useful not for the sake of winning arguments but for living as full a Christian life as possible. We are seeking to understand how baptism illustrates what is meant by faith and how faith relates to what is meant by baptism.

Put starkly: Did the early church baptize infants? "Early church" here would refer first to those believers whose doings and writings are included in New Testament documents. In an earlier chapter, we cited a number of "household" baptisms—stories of the merchant Lydia, the jailer at Philippi, a household at Corinth, and the like.

Some who cherish infant baptism and indulge in arguments about it go beyond the tantalizing but still inconclusive stories where baptisms occur and look in other texts where baptism is *not* mentioned. A favorite is the series of instances in which Jesus blessed children (Matt. 19:13-15; Mark 10:14-16; and Luke 18:15-17). I am not sure, however, that such an analogy can be used to make decisions by either side of the debate on infant baptism. Another text, 1 Corinthians 7:14, gets used by some to support infant baptism, but the case there is slim because it talks only about the holiness of children where one parent is a believer and the other is pagan.

Still others find a reasonable case for connecting baptism with the covenant of faith when they compare the baptism of infants to the practice of circumcising boys on their eighth day, as was the norm in the setting where Jesus lived and taught. Some churches found Paul's letter to the Colossians an appropriate reference, since it speaks of baptism as a circumcision: "In him also you were circumcised with a spiritual circumcision, by putting off the body of the flesh in the circumcision of Christ; when you were buried with him in baptism, you were also raised with him through faith in the power of God, who raised him from the dead" (2:11-12). Some theologians, however, are reluctant to make this comparison and thus question any relationship between the covenants of circumcision and baptism.

The biblical texts are frustratingly silent on the very questions on which the church of the past five centuries has wanted clarity. Lacking it, most Christian bodies have kept with what they saw most believers doing, unchallenged, from about the second to the sixteenth century—infant baptism.

While baptizers of infants speak of the impartation of grace through the sacrament, some add to this the motif of the covenant of grace and the discipline that goes with it. They therefore place everything on the weight of faith itself, as we noted above when we virtually equated justification by grace through faith with baptism. In the end, what matters is connecting the life of faith with baptism and, through baptism, connecting people at any age with the life of faith.

8

Baptism and Faith—
Faith and Baptism

CONNECTING FAITH with baptism and baptism with faith is one of the three most important "connections" we have to treat in a user's guide to baptism. The first important connection was that between "baptism" and "Word," for without the Word, emphatically, the water is only water. Second is the connection between baptism and water because with the Word, but only then, the water is a life-giving element, a tie to divine creation, a washing or "drowning" that provides the occasion for being resurrected with Christ. Having stressed those two, however, we have perhaps created some tension in the mind of you who read this, a tension that we want to address and, I hope, resolve creatively.

Nothing magical about baptism

The tension is there because we insist that there is nothing magical about the event of baptism. Recalling or turning to baptism daily, as we are urged do in repentance, serves as a reminder of what a gracious God has done for us. That is not magic; it is both a call for repentance and an act of repentance. That act means a turning-around, a complete turning away from "the old person" we were apart from Christ to realizing again, as we are to do each day, that we are now with Christ. While it sounds dangerous to say, in some scriptural contexts we are *a Christ to the neighbor.* As with all responses to grace in faith, Christians are privileged to respond with trust and resolve. All of these daily activities depend upon an act that the vast majority of Christians cannot recall having happened to them. Someone else brought them for baptism, spoke for them at baptism, and in many cases, either then forgot about the commitment or seldom reminded the growing child of the meaning of baptism. Deriving and experiencing grace as a result of an event that one cannot picture having experienced puts us in a chancy position, which we discussed earlier in connection with infant baptism.

Two approaches to baptism

As for those who baptize only those who have reached "the age of reason," whatever other faults or flaws these individuals or churches may have, they do not, or should not, have a problem with connecting baptism with faith. It may be that they have a somewhat different concept of what faith is than do those who baptize infants. So strong is their sense of this tie that many of them call their approach "believer's baptism."

The "believer's" reference is appropriate, though many who baptize infants hear it as somewhat insulting: do those who cherish that name for their approach consider infant baptizers to be engaging in "unbeliever's baptism?" Count me out of the company of the insulted, since I have read too many volumes full of insults and disparagements from both sides in the debates over believer's baptism to think that anything good could come out of a new round of hate e-mails and baptismal blogs on the Internet.

Rather, we can say some good things about those who take believer's baptism seriously. At their best, they are devoting themselves to the scriptural commands and promises as they understand them. If you are eighteen years old and have considered all the options but then chosen, against all odds and comfortable lures, to take up the call of Jesus Christ, you know what you are doing. Many who baptize only those who can speak for themselves and testify to the presence of faith before their baptism have come in range of our vision as people of faith who put to shame other Christians who have cared less than they do about justice, about ethics, about bringing the faith into the workplace or public order. Far be it for us to demean them.

So we have before us two ways, two versions of how to connect faith with baptism. What is the Christian to do? Most "do" without thinking. If you are in a culture where Baptists dominate and you are joining a Baptist church, you are tempted not to think things through, or you will find the act is so taken for granted that you do not have to think at all. If you are parents or other givers of care to infants in cultures where Catholics, Lutherans, Anglicans, Orthodox, and the vast majority of other Christians shape the ethos and customs, you unthinkingly do what everyone else does: bring infants for baptism. In this book, however, we are trying to avoid the automatic and unthinking approach and stopping to think through the consequence of baptism in both understandings.

Unless a divine voice pierces the clouds and settles the issue once and for all, we are likely to settle for two branches of Christianity on this point. Early in the years of the ecumenical movement, theologians grew tired of being told that if all communions simply followed the Bible they would all be one. Would that it was so easy!

Ecumenical scholars have observed from many gatherings how much of interpretation is shaped by what a reader brings to the text. Hand a mixed group of Baptists and Episcopalians the New Testament and ask them to settle this issue. A week, a year, a lifetime later, one is likely to observe people who are no longer wearing denominational labels such as Episcopal, Lutheran, Presbyterian, Catholic, or Baptist still being biased by their experience in these traditions. They will find in the New Testament books something that confirms what they were conditioned to find. They learn from each other. Anabaptists learn a thing or two about baptismal grace and infant baptizers learn about testimony and commitment. Yet when the day, or the year, is done, few will have moved across the line.

That paragraph may sound secular, off-putting, a good advertisement for remaining casual about books like this that aspire to be helpful and clear about baptism. Have we reached a "you pay your money and you take your choice" situation about the two approaches to baptism? I hope not. While acknowledging that there are things to learn from those who only practice believer's baptism, this book comes down on the side of infant baptism. In this chapter, then, we want to explore the benefits of connecting faith to the baptism of an infant, as the majority of Christians have done and still do. If we have this gift in our hands and consider it dangerous because it is so subject to misuse, then what are some of the ways we can use it to the glory of God, the benefit of humans, and, not least of all, for the deepening of our own faith?

Faith and infant baptism

What follows is an attempt to present, in orderly fashion, some themes that concentrate on the "faith-and-*infant*-baptism" issue only. I am going to take the step of borrowing from the work of Edmund Schlink, a scholar who devoted his long career to writing in systematic fashion about things of faith, and who published a whole book called *The Doctrine of Baptism* (St. Louis: Concordia, 1972). Schlink noticed that the historic confessions of his church put their weight on the church's response to the command of God. We will reproduce his thought as a basis for our own thought—and perhaps to whet the appetite for expanding the theme beyond the idea of obeying a divine command.

> The Holy Spirit, "placing us upon the bosom of the church . . . brings us to Christ." [Quoting the Large Catechism.] The faith of the church always precedes the faith of the individual.
>
> We do the same in infant Baptism. We bring the child with the purpose and hope that he may believe, and we pray God to grant him faith. But we do not baptize him on that account, but solely on the command of God. [Again, quoting the Large Catechism]. More than our "purpose" and "hope" that the person to be baptized may believe is in no case possible, not even in the case of an adult candidate for Baptism. Only God's command is

sure. . . . This command is, above all, the baptismal command which makes no exceptions. To this is added the Gospel selection used in Baptism, Mark 10:13-16: "Let the children come to me, do not hinder them. . . ." How then could we withhold Baptism from the children who are assured of the kingdom of heaven by Christ's invitation and Word? Is there something greater than the kingdom of heaven?

It is clear, therefore, that the benefit of Baptism and faith are inseparably conjoined. (153-54)

That passage is only the tantalizer, and Schlink was both tempted and expected to enlarge upon it, which he did twenty-one years later in his baptism book. He offered twelve theses that further connect baptism and faith before he commented on the consequences of this connection. My review will depend upon his sequence, but will not be confined to it; we have our own work to do.

To the point: first, we use infant baptism not only for its own sake, but to throw light on all biblical teaching and church practice as these relate to faith. Baptism, in this understanding, shines a spotlight on almost everything else one might want to say about faith. Properly conceived, it shows how to regard the human and divine relationship, and is one way of placing us before God so that we can realize the presence of God.

We have just read how baptism is connected to the Holy Spirit and the Christian church that does the baptizing. If it is so connected, believers have to take *very* seriously the testing of the faith of those who bring someone to be baptized and—isn't this scary?—they also have to take seriously the shape and condition of the faith of the church which is doing the baptizing.

The parents, pastors, and congregation cannot think of baptism as something that has been "done" for a child (or anyone else), but as a sacrament of God's holy call and promise, which expects a holy response.

Whether to baptize infants or not is something that many think can be settled by a coin toss of the church. Heads, we baptize. Tails, we wait for grown-ups to confess their faith and then we apply the Word and water sacramentally. No, *if* the church believes that baptizing infants is the correct way to respond to the encompassing command to baptize all, and if doing so is a sure way of showing this, then the church cannot *not* baptize the infant.

The children presented for baptism may have been brought by believing parents or by someone who takes on parental care-giving privileges and responsibilities. In either and all cases, when the church, acting under the Holy Spirit, receives a child for baptism, it is given the chance to proclaim to all who hear it that the child *needs* baptism.

No thoughtful person is going to ascribe sins to the baby or, acting as God's bookkeeper, will irrelevantly count the transgressions of the little one. So the child strains the parents' patience by crying as if in a willful, egocentric, shrieking tantrum. There is no need to register that as an evil that gives evidence of a wrong that we who baptize are to make right in baptism. Rather, in baptism we are proclaiming, as an order of baptism puts it, that "we are born children of a fallen humanity." Let the child grow and it will become evident that, even if she is a candidate for sainthood, there will be plenty of evidence that she does indeed belong to a fallen humanity. And, as such, before a holy God, she needs to be resituated in the new humanity that is reborn with the resurrection of Christ.

Often the baptizer will read a text that says "that which is born of the flesh is flesh, and that which is born of the Spirit is spirit" (John 3:6). If we Christians are "born children of a fallen humanity," we also follow these words with the phrase "by water and the Holy Spirit we are reborn children of God and made members of the church, the body of Christ."

At baptism, the church soon stops talking about sinful humanity and moves on to proclaim the great good news that God wants all people to be saved by being "joined . . . to the death and resurrection of our Lord Jesus Christ," and that now, ahead of us, is the fact that "we grow in faith, love, and obedience to the will of God." Nothing throws into more vivid and searching light the faith that ascribes *all* to God's activity. When the gospel is read and believed, or when it quotes Jesus' command and request to let the children come to him "for of such is the kingdom of God," the baptizing church proclaims that God's reach and rescue operation includes children. The gospel announces that Jesus accepts children long before they reach the age of reason and consent. Baptism is for them.

Baptism, in this understanding, is not a vaccination so much as it is a call up to service, something like a military draft. That is, baptism is not something "done" to inoculate a baby to grow up untouched by temptation and given a free ride through a stormy life, with God standing by to provide pats on the back. Instead the child is given over to the one who was killed on the cross and raised from the dead, Jesus Christ, with whom forever the growing person is identified in suffering and glory. On baptismal day, it is made clear that God is not a one-day wonder-worker but a receiver into the divine embrace in which we are comforted, and from which we are also impelled into a world where the love of God is to be put to work.

Another feature of baptismal faith is its connection with what faith has to draw upon, namely, the quest for truth. When Jesus is self-identified in the gospel as "the truth," the evangelist is not portraying him as a living encyclopedia in which all the little truths add up to one big Truth. Instead, this truth of faith is less about "what you know" and more about "who you know."

The baptismal service does not say, "Today we commit this child to learning 364 answers to questions in the catechism," or "Today we launch another infant on a career toward a Ph.D. in theology so he is ready for the kingdom." The spoken Word at baptism is rather about a rich approach to a full life under God and in Christ, as guided by the Holy Spirit. When today or tonight you make the sign of the cross upon arising or going to bed, you are marking another step along the way in which the truth of God unfolds in the lifelong development of a Christian person.

No one expects the infant to realize intellectually that she is now a member of the church. If church is thought of as an organization, to mention being a member of it would imply that in next week's mail the child would get a packet of offering envelopes so she can begin to take a responsible role in stewardship. No one expects her to read and follow the local church calendar or support the works of mercy that the church at its best undertakes. However, the baptizers and the receiving church are signaling that the child is now a member, with the benefits that come with God's promises, long before congregational life and churchly participation imply a call. Let teens fight temptation and enjoy some victories. Let church professionals wrestle over the meaning of their call. Let people of strength and wisdom summon resources to fight off an assaulting and tempting world. The child on her baptismal day is being committed to take part in all that through all the developing stages of life. Not yet. Instead, the child, held up—some baptizing pastors physically lift up this "newest member" for all to see—symbolizes the helplessness that all penitent Christians of all ages have to feel along with their trust and creative dependence upon God for strength, as Jesus demonstrates in his scenes with children.

The baptismal service and event are also connected with faith as shown by the heavy reliance on prayer. When a child is received into the Boys and Girls Club or becomes a citizen along with immigrant parents, no prayer is prescribed or expected. Many may choose to pray, of course, but prayer is not part of the order of service on such occasions. In the service of baptism, however, as we have heard, the pastor gives thanks at the font:

> We give you thanks, O God. . . . [Now] pour out your Holy Spirit, the power of your living Word, that those who are washed in the water of baptism may be given new life.

And after the baptism:

> We give you thanks, O God, that through water and the Holy Spirit you give your daughters and sons new birth.

Then with his or her hand on the head of the newly baptized, the presider prays for:

> the spirit of wisdom and understanding, the spirit of counsel and might, the spirit of knowledge and the fear of the Lord, the spirit of joy in your presence, both now and forever. (ELW, 230-231)

Looking ahead, as we may and must, and with the prayers that look ahead with the whole of life in mind, it is important to note that the body that was just washed is the body that someday will be laid to rest. And so we are told:

When we were baptized in Christ Jesus, we were baptized into his death. We were buried therefore with him by baptism into death, so that as Christ was raised from the dead by the glory of the Father, we too might live a new life. For if we have been united with him in a death like this, we shall certainly be united with him in a resurrection like his. (ELW, 280)

Connecting baptism with death in order to connect it with faith in the resurrection may not be the choice of everyone when a beautiful baby's early life is being celebrated. But baptism is for every day and all the days—unto and then beyond death.

Many in our culture work strenuously to avoid thinking about death. The famous physician Dr. Lewis Thomas liked to urge serious people not to deny it but to think about and talk about death, because, as he said, "there's a lot of it going around these days!" To be brutally open about it, one wag defined life itself as "a sexually-transmitted disease with a terminal prognosis." To the contrary, in baptism we say that this *new life* is a divinely transmitted cure with an expectation of eternal life.

Given the child's utter dependence and weakness, when connecting baptism and faith, the church has a special occasion to demonstrate and to celebrate divine power. God is working in and through that child to reach those who surround him now, will nurture him later, and will interact with him, one hopes, lifelong in the exercising of justice and mercy. God chooses the weak, Paul the apostle wrote. So who better to choose for witnesses than the infants? Compare notes with those who love and learn from children and many of them will testify to the fact that they learned the love of God through the interactive expressions of love between an infant and parents. One does not have to be baptized or be a baptizer to receive a child's love. In baptism, however, there is a new impulse for seeing the love and power of God afresh.

Here is still another feature of life that both occurs and is witnessed to in the baptism of infants: almost all other acts of response and reception among believers can include an admixture of self-congratulations. "I did it, God. You owe me blessings. In faith, I tithed. In faith, I served on committees, wrapped cancer bandages, carried meals on wheels to the aged, spoke up for you in a campus intellectual tussle. It's time you noticed me and pinned 'Congratulations' on my coat." But in baptism, it is all about God—not the one baptized. In infant baptism, this poor and weak receiver of grace is, without trying to do so, preaching an eloquent sermon about divine generosity.

A moment ago we connected the baptism of an infant with the fulfilling of her life up to and then beyond death. Along with that, connecting faith and baptism helps us teach a whole new approach to temporal life, to the chronology we are used to, as when we say, "When she grows up . . ." "Now that we are mature . . ." "I'm glad to have survived a midlife crisis . . ." "It's been a good run . . ." "Now that autumn or the evening of life is coming on . . ." "Be with us as the shadows lengthen and the evening comes and the busy world is hushed, the fever of life is over, and our work is done. . . ."

In our imagination and habitual thinking we have that order of the ages and stages of life all determined. And here comes baptism to mess it all up. The end of life is here, already in the beginning. The promised rest gets realized now when you retire at night, having made the sign of the cross. Unforeseen crises of health or meaning will come to everyone, but the baptized child is made ready for dealing with crisis by not having to deal with crisis: it is left in God's hand.

Most important, the baptized one has already experienced death, the death that in God's sight matters most. The baptized is three weeks old in the old life but new as each day in the new life. The hourglass gets tipped, the diary pages turned around, the calendar found to be useless in the life of faith: it is all here, now, at the beginning. A baptized person can opt out, pay no attention, and move toward spiritual death. All the while, the seal of baptism stands as a daily call and promise of God.

Baptism and the community of faith

Since so much is at stake and so many meanings are involved, a church that has integrity baptizes only those who bring the child in faith to the circle of the committed faithful, the church. Add it all up and note that the church in baptizing infants is confident that the Christian community is following the divine command and responding to God's promise.

Baptism is not something that just happens to the one or three children gathered at the font. It is an act of confession and commitment by everyone present. We recall that in baptism it is the church and the faith of the church that are being witnessed to and are serving as witnesses. The child later can make all kinds of wrong decisions or can forget the promises, but the promises of baptism come without strings attached. In fact, no other ritual, act, gesture, proposition, or movement of the church so splendidly condenses all that is taught and believed about how God the Holy Spirit works and sustains faith as does infant baptism. The church is never healthier than when it has nothing to depend upon but the promises of God. Baptism illustrates that, and, for the persons involved, it effects the promises.

If this interpretation of the command and promises of God and the faith and commitment of the church are true to baptism, it will become clearer again why we have spoken of the blessings of baptism in the context of danger, of perilous activity, and confession. The baptizing church has the responsibility of seeing to it that baptism is not a routine on the one hand or a magic act on the other. The counseling that ought to go on as parents or adult individuals ponder baptism should include education and a call to commitment. If not, the connection between baptism and faith may be broken and all that remains is baptism and custom, baptism and habit, baptism and social pressure, baptism and family reunions, baptism and commerce.

The counselor, teacher, or preparer, of course, has to be, and in grace will be, generous in interpreting all of this. Pre-baptism is not the time to be arrogant about what "we" have by way of truth before God and what "you" and "those" who are casual do not have. It is not the time to narrow the borders, raise the fences, or slam the door on others. Often church leaders can discern ways in which the bringing of children to baptism is a first step in the path to membership and discipleship. The baptizer can make some mistakes, can misread the signals that parents and other caregivers bring. But in the delicate balance between the will to please families on the one hand and to help make clear the meaning and purpose of baptism on the other, the minister can act in trust that God will cover for mistakes and miscalculations. When in doubt, the church, through its pastors, teachers, and counselors, should err on the side of being generous, with all the risks that go with it, and with the hope that those who present someone for baptism will take their promises seriously, grow in faith, and be responsible—rather than make the church seem like a know-it-all or a Grand Inquisitor. Preparation for baptism is a wonderful teaching opportunity for a take-risk church; it also has the potential for destroying relations and harming the very church that would like to participate in healing.

What is necessary is a program of attention to the meaning of baptism and the disciplines that go with it. Those who desire the baptism of someone else should desire it in faith, but they will not know to do this if there is a disconnect between faith and baptism as these are lived out in the culture. Almost nothing in the culture will be on the side of those who want baptism to be faithful to Christ's command or to be more than something that is merely "done," or that would be nice, or that wouldn't hurt, or that would please parents-in-law. Regular teaching and preaching will help in this turn-around. Active members of churches conversing with the less active or the occasional drop-ins who are likely to come by for a one-shot approach to baptism will aid.

Some not-so-persuasive defenses of infant baptism

In our effort to relate the grace of God for infants through baptism in connection with faith, we have stressed only one element: the faith of the church and the working of the Holy Spirit through life in the body of Christ. Doing so means paying little attention to the many kinds of other arguments adduced by defenders of infant baptism in a time when such baptism is so often corrupted or misunderstood. Some defenders of infant baptism will find a few of the following ideas convincing, or at least half-convincing, but most of the debating points are too contrived and chancy to bear much weight. Still, they should be entered into the record, and discussion of them belongs in any sustained examination of baptism among responsible church people in our pluralistic culture. Without developing any to great extent, let me cite them:

- Some defenders of infant baptism turn psychologist and contend that the experience of baptism is somehow sense-experienced by a baby, and that nurture later on can build on this. Many psychologists say that with the recognition of a smile by the mother, an infant receives a first sign of warmth in the cold universe into which that infant has been thrown by being born. Can it, therefore, not be that the child is aware of what is going on in the earliest weeks of life, and can build on that in the development of faith?

- Modern psychologists do tend to see more in early childhood experience than most did formerly, but the leaps one must make to picture that anything an infant hears can be a summons to faith, a call to obedience, an assurance of promise, transcends all the findings in this field. Splash cold water on the infant and she will react, but she does not yet have any developed capacity to interpret what is going on. Slam a book shut loudly near a child and he will jump in reaction. Yet the gap between water and the water of baptism, or the noise and reading of the Word of God at baptism is too large to breach. We will forget it.

- Some like to claim, often with bits of warrant from the Christian past, that in baptism faith is being injected or infused into the child; they even had a Latin name for it: *fides infantilis*, which also was seen to be an image of mother love. The mother shows love, and the child picks up on it and can develop love the rest of her life.

- A third set of apologists sees infant baptism as a kind of well-placed bet, a wager, because the baptizers do their act in the prospect of faith that will *someday* be born in the person. Since such faith follows baptism, it does not connect with baptism, and therefore is not really about baptism at all, and thus is not helpful on the present point.

- One of the most popular approaches has a slight New Testament basis in stories where Jesus saw "their faith," meaning the faith of others, and then acted favorably toward the one with whom the others are associated. When Jesus saw the faith of those who lowered a paralyzed man through the roof, he turned and favorably regarded the victim who needed healing. Regular churchgoers have heard sermons on "the kind of faith that saves others." They refer to people like the patient mother Monica who prayed for her son's conversion and baptism so strenuously and regularly that God, she thought, had to notice and work faith in her son, Augustine. So in our time, the faith of Aunt Myrna, who is a godmother, is seen to have some carry over to the child. Some would call this "faith by representation" or "vicarious faith." What is meant by faith in this context, however, is different from the kind of faith associated with baptism.

- Some do not bother to think very deeply beyond considering that "whatever is, is right." "Everybody does it," so who are we to question what the church for almost two millennia has been doing and thinking? They must have seen something in baptism, or implanted something into it, that we dare not lightly disturb. No reformer of the church, however, would buy this one, since reform always has to be ready to mean a breaking up of what was already there. The church in the long past carried on crusades and inquisitions, engaged in forced conversions, or allied itself with the state. No more. Each generation has to ask afresh what it is to understand, and not just accept things as they are.

- Other defenses are based in analogies that don't work. Recall that in an analogy there is some difference in every sameness and some sameness in every difference. So far, so good, but there can be failed analogies. So we read on occasion that when immigrant parents pass citizenship examinations and take an oath to support the constitution, the tots come right along with them. They get civil rights along with their parents' civil rights. So the sameness lies in that in both cases there are parents, children, promises, and pledges. The meaning of citizenship as a free ride and baptism as free passage, by themselves, are insufficient. Furthermore, such an analogy takes away from Christian understandings of the church and the role of the children of the baptized within it.

Large volumes, if not libraries, have been filled with attacks on and defenses of infant baptism. They tend to convince the convinced and drive away those who began far off. This is not to say that there is never to be exploration, never discovery, never debate. Rather it is to note that few are won over by arguments on either side, and that the church in its various branches should explore and teach how to live with the conception of baptism that is current and available while exposing the group that holds the concept to the wide range of ways to be a Christian.

9

⎯⎯⎯◦⟨◦⟩◦⎯⎯⎯

User's Guide to Baptism

IN THIS FINAL CHAPTER, we will drop any suggestion that this book is only a discussion in the third person about baptism, an approach designed to teach something about biblical, historical, and theological themes devoted to baptism. We now turn the page to a consistent first- and second-person discussion, full of the language of "I" or "we" and "you."

This being a user's guide, I have tried to imagine the interests of persons and parties who are immediately involved with baptism. However, I plead with readers who do not see themselves in a particular category—for example, we cannot really get into the mind of a three-week-old child—to read on and share in the imagining. All through these pages, I hope that we will be teaching and learning more about baptism in ways that *do* affect us all.

To adults being baptized—and everyone else

To be read by any adult who is considering baptism, is already baptized, is being baptized, or who wants to learn about baptism—as well as by relatives, congregants, baptizers, pastors, evangelists, and the merely curious. The section ahead will take the form of a virtual letter, a form that allows for a more personal and committed tone than would most anything written in the third person. The intention is to help users prepare for their roles relating to baptism, as well as help those who will use it to learn or review what is involved with baptism.

Go therefore and make disciples of all nations, baptizing them. Matthew 28:19

Dear prospect for baptism:

The dictionaries are beginning to allow us to call you a "baptizee." You may not think of yourself as a baptizee, because you have not heard the word. My hugest dictionary gives it one line and marks it rare. To the dictionary writer, it means someone who "is a recipient of baptism." Since we are resurrecting the word and giving it new life, we can also provide fresh meaning by using it to refer to someone who is planning to be baptized or about to be baptized.

In the early Christian church you might well have been called a "catechumen," someone who is being catechized, a word that refers to a method of teaching through formal questions and answers. That word shows up in the term *missa catechumenorum*, which was the mass of Holy Communion for those being catechized; that is, those who were becoming candidates for baptism. You might well not have enjoyed being assigned to that status, since the word appears over against the *missa fidelium*, which is the mass for "the faithful," those who were already baptized and who live in the grace of their baptism.

Some of the reasons for excluding you from the *missa fidelium* back when the church was being persecuted are not as compelling or urgent today. Back then, the believers were under suspicion, and they did not want to risk being exposed either for engaging in magic or, in the eyes of many Romans, engaging in a subversive rite. You can't blame the Roman government and the neighbors down the block for being suspicious. Rumors were out in some circles at the time that you were cannibals, "eating your god." After all, the administrator of the Lord's Supper invited believers to "take and eat" the bread for it was the body of Christ and to "take and drink" the wine for it was the blood of Christ. Eating bread and drinking wine sounded savage, or at least confusing. It was confusing because some of the cults in the Roman world did engage in extreme ceremonies, and it was easy for unbelievers to place Christians in their company.

Closing the door, then, was not a bad idea when it occurred in order to exclude the ignorant, the curious, the not-yet-fully convinced, snoopy neighbors who might be enemies, and those we might think of as plainclothesmen spying for the authorities. Baptism today can also occur in dangerous circumstances, as we have reasons to remind ourselves, but most readers of this book, when baptized as adults, do not have their story written up in the newspapers, and what they are doing will be at best cheered or at worst ignored by neighbors.

Odds are that you have given thought to what is about to happen in your baptism. That you can give thought is one reason why we, who baptize infants and practice a faith that grows out of the grace associated with infant baptism, might have a tinge of envy for you who are being baptized as adults and thus have had reason and opportunity to deliberate this act and commitment. We hope that your preparation for baptism was strenuous, at least as demanding as classes at night school where you or those around you were learning a trade or preparing for a profession. Such formal Christian teaching is not so much an introduction to "what you know" as it is a deeper commitment to "whom you know," namely God, here realized as God in Christ.

Such teaching might involve some study of the Apostolic and Nicene Creeds, details of which keep theological students busy for three or four years and, we hope, will occupy you for at least three or four short hours. Along with presenting the creeds, a good teacher will stress and sample teachings in the sacred scriptures, especially those that bear on themes such as baptism, faith, grace, covenant, congregation, commitment, and ethics, which here means good ways of life. Being realists, we who teach do not picture this study as a seminary education. But we also know that there is no other moment in adult life in which motivation will be so strong as now to learn what baptism is and means; no better time to learn what God's commitment to you is and to learn what you are committing yourself to in grace-filled response.

We have to press this teaching-and-learning issue for two reasons. First, in our culture many parents bring their children for the rite of baptism and then in forgetfulness or ignorance do nothing about it. Such children then join the millions of others who grow up knowing little or nothing and doing less than nothing about baptism. They hardly stand out from the unbaptized and fail to receive the benefits that come with baptism.

Since so many of your contemporaries were baptized in infancy, most adults who "join the church" will not remember the originating act of baptism. They are conventionally received by affirming their unremembered baptism of long ago. This means that in many a congregation one can belong for years or even decades and not be present at an adult baptism. (That sentence could be read as an admonition to believers to get busy and carry on the mission of the church; it implicitly urges us to "go" and present the faith so that the un-baptized will become engaged and may seek to be born again or born from above by washing in the water of life in the kingdom of God.)

If you are a candidate for baptism in parts of America or Europe you may be a rare figure, standing alone in front of a baptizing assembly of Christians. However, you would not be exceptional if you lived in sub-Saharan Africa, on the subcontinent of Asia, or in the Pacific Island world where every Sunday many thousands of adult converts will be baptized. Your baptism in such places, if the climate is warm, might well occur under a thatched-roofed chapel built without obscuring walls, so that the crowds can spill out into the surrounding area. Or in other places you might make the trip to whatever passes for the Jordan River, or a pond, and your baptism will remind congregants of the story of Jesus' baptism. The gathering would enjoy a festive meal after your baptism and first communion, and your catechists, pastors, baptizers, some elders, and families will be cheering you on. You will never forget the day, nor will those who support you.

The second reason for making so much of the teaching-and-learning is that as an adult baptizee you can, if you are informed, be a witness to those around you who lack the grace that comes with the baptismal word and experience. You might be a shy person and no one expects you to say more than the prescribed responses in the baptismal service. The one who is baptizing will feed the words to you in a "repeat after me" format, or you can have the service book open before you.

Most of the time, those who do the baptizing will not expect a shy adult to present his or her statement of faith to a congregation likely made up of people who are still strangers to the person being baptized. Still, if you are someone who is able and willing to speak for yourself, and I hope you will be, the congregation will be "all ears" and its members will cheer you on.

What you might say on such an occasion can inform and inspire others. Since you are not being baptized in order to become a public orator, the congregation will not expect to hear a polished declaration of faith. However, over coffee, in adult classes, or in common activities of your faith community, you might be asked—and will be ready to explain—what went into your reception of grace and your readiness to make a commitment. And since you are not here in person to speak up, let me envision a couple of scenarios that distill some of what might be said at such times.

Much common witness, we presume, would come from adults who are going to marry a committed Christian, or from someone who has been married but has remained somewhat distant spiritually from a spouse who is baptized. Let's picture this scene set within a marriage. At the time of the marriage you two may have talked seriously about faith, but you also had other things on your mind to cause you to defer further talk. That original distance between you two either grew and became a problem for communication or it narrowed and you were ready to take up the old theme. You read some books about the faith, probably attended worship with your spouse, or perhaps went through a crisis in which Christian faith could have been a resource. At any rate, somewhere along the way you said that you were ready; you took instruction, and planned for baptism. If others in your circle or congregation are at the same stage as you, the pastor or other leader may encourage you to be baptized with others—for example, on the night before Easter. As an adult baptizee, you become a living witness to baptism as it has been practiced for almost twenty centuries.

We profit from envisioning baptisms of long ago. Because civil authorities were not favorable to baptism, you and your fellow believers may well be gathering out of sight, sometimes in caves or in the underground of a city, usually near a stream or where living water bubbles up. It is dark, and shadows remain through much of the evening while your fellow believers sing hymns and recite scriptures. Later, enough light is brought in for the baptism. You are plunged into flowing water or a cistern, or you are washed with the pouring of water from vessels that are on hand.

After the baptism, more lights are brought in as you greet each other with the words, "Christ is risen!" "He is risen indeed!" How daring, how romantic, how unforgettable, one is allowed to think, because baptism in such circumstances was challenging and thus most memorable. Your spiritual ancestors walked away from the ceremony with no visible marks on their bodies. The water soon evaporated, the oil in the lamps ran out, the sun came up and you had things to do both on this Lord's Day and on the days that followed, days when you got a chance to see your faith develop, both ordinary days and extraordinary days when the tests of faith and the needs for baptismal grace only grew.

As you prepare for baptism, it is good to remember that persecution goes on in our own time as well. As already mentioned, yearbooks of the churches regularly point to the fact that many Christians suffer and die for their faith each year within our world of jealous oppressors. What a difference from that to what will most likely happen on your own baptismal day. It may occur in a tiny chapel or a country church from whose location many have moved away. Or you could receive the sacrament in the baptistry of a splendid cathedral or a college chapel. The "where" offers limitless choices. All you need wherever it may be, are water, an ear for the Word that is integral to every baptism, and an open heart. And like those who live in persecution, you too will need the courage to *live in* your baptismal commitments.

While you are reading this to prepare for baptism, think about how your baptism connects you with the mission of the church. Recall that the prescription for baptism, according to the gospels, was heard in Jesus' words at the very end of the gospel. He has taken care of all needs—bringing you in growing faith to the community of faith, where you are aware of your sins and recognize your soul's hunger. But, one learns from the scriptures, Jesus is mindful—as he wants you to be—that most humans are not yet part of that community. They are unaware of their sins and do not know what do to with and about them or how to have their souls fed. And here you are, having explored your own shortcomings but having become aware of God's loving reach. And you hear the word, "go therefore and make disciples of all nations." It is the mission of the church and will be your mission.

Have you thought of this: that you are as equipped for the task as the original disciples were? You have the basics of Christian knowledge in reach, and while you do not have the living presence of the human Jesus, you do have an awareness of his divine presence thanks to the work of the Holy Spirit. You have learned of Jesus' promise that wherever and whenever two or three believers are gathered in his name, he will be there with them. In baptism you take up life in company with other believers—and Jesus is there with you.

You may not literally go into all nations, though many thousands of believers like you do go many thousands of miles beyond what Jesus' disciples could have envisioned. Odds are that representatives of "all nations" now live down the block or up the road from you, thanks to immigration policies that bring in unbaptized and religiously uncommitted people from all over the world. In spite of the fact that most people in our culture assure pollsters that they are spiritual or that they believe in God, we observe many who have not begun in faith and have not yet taken advantage of God's offer.

You, dear candidate for baptism, with your fresh experience of learning, deciding to be baptized, and coming to know its benefits in faith, can approach others who are less aware of those benefits. And in a culture where so many take church participation so lightly, or the struggle of faith so lackadaisically, you can be in the advance guard of a recovering church that is hearing again the call to "make disciples."

We are not likely to have such thoughts when the baptized person is a baby, but you are an adult, and so it is up to you to seize the opportunities that are given to you to help fire up more casual believers who live in a time when faith cannot be taken for granted in the larger society. Thanks for giving us the impetus by your presence and your witness to the Christian faith as you respond to the baptizer.

Baptism is about you but it is not only about you. It is an act of the larger Christian community around the globe. Remember that today you are joining in a ministry to others, becoming a member in the "priesthood of believers," and becoming a part of a special people who are equipped to serve the purposes of God in their lives—lives that earlier may have lacked purpose.

We said earlier that there are no visible marks that come with baptism once the water has dried; however, in a profound way, you, your body, your ways, and your life together become visible marks for the world to see. You will be baptized "into Christ," will "put on Christ," and are to see Christ in your neighbor even as you become a Christ for your neighbor. You are being "anointed" (which is what the name "Christ" means) so that you can enjoy the benefits of faith and take on the obligations that go with your commitment.

One last thing belongs in this letter: while you will be full of resolve and gifted with new energies from the Holy Spirit, by the evening of your baptism enough will have gone on to remind you that you are not a finished product. To put it frankly, by the end of the day you will have sinned and, we hope, will have become aware of that, and of how it offended God, the people around you, and your own self which has been enriched with new resolves. If you have no intellectual grasp of how you will need baptismal grace daily, then we will have wasted your time with this book. If like many believers, however, you have such a grasp, you will now know what to do with your shortcomings: repent and continue living in the grace, gifts, and obligations of your baptism.

Therefore, on the morning after your baptism, you *get* to wake up to a new messy day. For the first time, on that morrow, you get to make the sign of the cross as a means of signing and recalling the fact of your baptism and the receipt of its promise. In scriptural terms, you *get* to walk in newness of life. Thanks for helping us understand the meaning of that walk for the sake of our own tomorrows.

A letter for an infant being baptized—to be opened someday

While this appears bound between the covers of a book, I ask you to picture it as a kind of letter set aside for an infant until she is grown.

We can't wait that long to get its message, however, so we will peek at it. And our hurry is the consequence of our awareness that every Christian who knows a typical baptized child assumes some obligations and enjoys some privileges. We could only picture a limited number of children, but we know that they arrive and grow in all sorts of circumstances, and that by putting ourselves in the place of the child, we may learn much about the marvelous variety of little members of the kingdom of God. This is a reminiscence of how things were for a child who could not have been aware of them "back then," but who may be curious about how it was—and what it means now. If you are not a child, you may be tempted to pass it by. Please look: it's intended also for you.

Dear baptized child of God:

Some years ago someone, probably your parents, brought you to baptism. Since we are preparing a little packet to be tucked away with baptismal certificates and baby pictures for any number of infants, we can do no more than envision you now growing or even grown in your particular context. From what we know of the church around the world, we are free to do some imagining and picturing, and doing so may give you and those who bring you up more reasons to appreciate your baptism and their call to nurture you in faith. So, imagine this as we try to picture you.

- You may have been a baby found under a tree in Africa or an abandoned child found on a back porch in the city, one whose biological parents we may never know, someone who is "nobody's child," but who became a child of God because someone presented you for baptism, promised to care for you, and still does care.
- You may be growing up as a child of a couple who are members of a Christian congregation, a devoted pair

who prayed that you be conceived and born. You are especially precious to them, because you were a long time coming and you had a hard time being born, but thanks to what modern medicine can do, you became healthy, and were able to squawk loudly and kick your feet lustily during your baptism. The congregation could hardly hear the words that day, but they were spoken, and believed, and everyone rejoiced that you had lungs with which to bellow, not to peep. You have needed much medical care, but on lonely nights and uncertain mornings, those who cared for you prayed with confidence in the name of the Son of God to favor you as a little child of God.

- You may be the child of a single mother who did not plan to have you but was graced to bring you to term and see you born. You have found that she was under considerable stress all along, burdened by guilt and full of fear but also from the first full of love for you. She was in less of a position than were some others to teach you the prayers and guide your way. You were blessed, however, with grandparents who stepped in and helped lift her load until she matured. They summoned other relatives and friends to surround you, and these helped set you right, too, when that was needed through the early years of your life. She is now married and you, your stepfather, your sister, and your friends can look forward to good years for you, one day at a time.

- You may have been adopted by parents who are Christian and who took it as a solemn obligation and a happy opportunity to bring you to the font for baptism. Yours was an "open adoption" and your birth mother, who could not take on the task of nurturing you, was happy to know that the spiritual side of your upbringing was being taken care of. And as you grow and know in more detailed and vivid ways what being adopted means, you can be a living parable to others, showing what it means that all believers are adopted into God's family. It may be that your parents have told you that other children "just happened," whereas you were "chosen." Those who talk that way do not want to minimize the wonder of child-bearing, but to remind you of the wonders of being adopted—as we all are as children of God, brothers and sisters of Christ.

- You may have been brought to baptism by parents who, at grandparents' urging, finally agreed to please them by having you baptized. Grandpa and Grandma, whom you have come to love, were not content to see your baptism as something that "is done," merely to have you "christened" so that you would not stand out and be embarrassed in a part of a culture where so many other children are baptized. So by example, as they brought you to church and church school, they taught you prayers, and, without being meddling busybodies, set examples that helped produce the happy person you have become. They won your parents over to the idea of investing your baptism with new meanings. Now, instead of being casual and lazy Christians in name only, they have, through your presence, learned to express their own faith and to draw on their own baptisms, whose meaning they had largely forgotten back when you were born.

Enough samples of imagining. Before we seal this packet for annual opening we want to comment on some other features of baptism when babies are concerned. Here are a few.

First, think of your baptism as being a gift into which you will grow. On one level, baptism is a finished product. As a tiny child you didn't need any more than the water of baptism with the Word of God that makes it a sacrament or holy act, and the promise that goes with faith. On another level, the consequences of baptism are anything but complete, and they won't be seventy or eighty years from now either when your life nears its end. In this way of picturing life, think of your baptism as a beautiful jewel, like one a woman might wear, a woman who appears to be more beautiful because of the beauty that adorns her. She acquires a new image of herself, one that helps her become a more attractive person. Attractive here need not mean physical beauty. There are many ways to be attractive. But you have seen already in your few years how people can change, often for the better, and you are learning what your baptism and its promises can contribute to your development. They will inspire you to enjoy the lifelong search and the constant finding of, or being found by, God.

If the older people who surround you are doing a good job of bringing you up baptismally, you also will have learned, and will learn more of, your need for God's help. They probably have read books that described the newborn as "innocent" and then joked that it was hard to see that innocence as their own child grew. Your little Jewish friends, by the way, are not seen as sinners until they are of age to learn the law of God, as when they prepare for bar mitzvah or bat mitzvah. That makes good sense in Judaism. But, while adult Christians cannot expect you to know in detail all the right-and-wrong contexts and acts, they and you learn pretty soon that you can go astray. You have seen or may have been in fights on the playground. You can as a brother or sister beat each other up in order to monopolize a toy. You have shown selfishness and have not always been generous. However, you have been taught with your bedtime prayers to approach God not as a "bad kid" who does "bad things" but as a child of God, named with Jesus, forgiven, and given a new start each day.

That new start helps you form a good life. In adult language, we speak of "ethics," having and using a system in which you set and follow a positive pattern of life that we associate with baptismal grace. Certainly, by now, you will have been taught the Ten Commandments, and have tried to be obedient. Less certainly, but more importantly, you are to be taught that the baptized child who is having a hard time following the commandments is to be forgiven when forgiveness is sought. Equally important, you are to learn what it means to be moved by the love of Jesus to show what being a child of God means. This is the case when it comes to relating to family and friends as well as when you begin to make up your mind about how to feed the hungry, clothe the naked, and get to do all the other things that Jesus in the gospels told you to do.

We don't picture that any time you get into trouble you can get out of trouble by running around saying, "You can't touch me: I'm baptized!" That would get you nowhere, because it would take what is to be a heartfelt desire to do better and turn it into something mechanical. When you are in trouble, however, you are using your baptism when you show that you know where to turn and what to do about being set right. The meanings of baptism tell you that better than anything else.

Back on your baptismal day, everyone made a fuss over you. You wore grandmother's baptismal dress, were posed for pictures, and got passed around at the family's baptism dinner. It took some hard knocks later for you to learn that the universe is not built around you. You didn't acquire a license to turn in upon yourself and make everyone bow to you. You did acquire the instruments and materials to help you remain aware of what being God's child means, and to connect it with baptism and its audacious promises.

Everyone knows what a problem child is said to be: all that he is or does creates problems for those who deal with him. While not every boy or girl gets classified as a "problem child," great numbers do have problems. To begin a description of a child around problems reduces the child to being "nothing but autistic" or "nothing but delinquent." Baptism is a mystery that throws a child like you into the boundless setting of unfathomable mystery, into new depths, where imagination and curiosity, wonder and play are dominant. So, child, when we say that you have depths that cannot be explained away, we speak of your baptism and you as mysteries.

Thinking about that little bit of water and some promises made by parents and godparents can lead to confusion. Yet you, child, by the way you are receptive, responsive, and open to the call of God and others will be given grace to live joyfully in the context of mystery. Your parents do not have to be perfect to bring you up. It is reasonable to picture them sometimes losing patience, not pretending that they are God. They also were baptized and have needed to return to their baptism in thought and resolve. Then they can let you, dear child, *be* and be brought up with discipline that is reinforced by love. Some of these ideas and some of this language might pass you by right now, as these paragraphs did when you were tiny and new. But we enter it into the record so you can grow in understanding as this is read and explained to you.

Years have passed since your parents stored your baptismal clothes, but they have kept the reality of your baptism alive, and will never "store" it. Whenever they pray for you, often when they correct you, and always when they inspire you, they are building upon the baptism, which made you a child of God. Having God as their partner and mentor in bringing you up was and is good for them and for you. You are part of a family, no matter whether you are at times distant from one of your parents or even if one of them scolds you too harshly. Baptism is a way God uses to show you that you will never be abandoned.

At school and with friends you will often meet children to whom none of this makes sense. They probably do not go to church. Their parents might say they can worship God during a walk in the woods or in a canoe on a lake. They have been taught to tell you that church is just a club where the dues are high and leaders are always talking about money. Some of them have heard the horrifying stories of youth ministers or priests who have done evil things to children under their care, and they have difficulty even thinking about how damaging that is or bringing up the subject to you. But remember, your baptizing community creates a setting where *you can* bring up problems of trust and faith.

Baptism, as your godparents can tell you, was destined to make it possible for you to live a full spiritual life. We hope that as you come to know the love of God that comes with this life and what it signifies, you will grow up to be a care-free, open-minded child full of a spirit of wonder and adventure. All this should be a part of baptismal faith, a faith that tells you that the God who made you cares for you and cares about you, and that you get to serve this God and the world with its people whom God created and loves.

One final word: every year on the anniversary of your baptism those who care for you might throw a little party. It is the date of your "second birth." Sometimes they might take you out to a fun restaurant; other times they might invite your godparents and a few others over to celebrate your being a child of God. A couple of years ago they described to you all about your baptismal day: how the sun shone or the rain fell, how the church was half-full but the voices of those that were there were full of praise and thanks to God for you. That was just one of the many ways your family helped make use of your baptism so that you realize the benefits and joys that came with it.

Now, it would be helpful if you studied your Bible so that in a future Sunday school class or confirmation session you will not simply know what was in the assignment but will better know Jesus, the one who will help you to learn and to live his way.

To you parents, of course

No group of potential readers has more at stake than the parents of a child who is to be baptized, is baptized, or who was baptized and whose status now has to be understood. Since the parents are representatives of the child and, in a way, of the congregation, we all, parents or not, have reason to wrestle with and delight in their responsibilities and joys. Once again, we include some elements of baptismal doctrine and practice, which we think will imply and inform all readers.

Dear parents of a baptized child or a child to be baptized:

Presenting a child in baptism, as you have done or will do, often evokes rather conventional images. Motion pictures and other media of both church and culture tend to place baptisms in modified Gothic or discreetly modern sanctuaries filled with people. In front of the congregation a minister poses in clerical garb. Near the baptismal font are a couple of officiants who will provide a candle, perhaps some oil, a certificate, and a symbol of congregational involvement. Around the font or pool are children of the congregation who have natural curiosity about what is going on and are open to learning. There are usually two godparents. Family members, equipped with cameras, fill the front pews. In the center at the font are a man and a woman. She or the godmother is holding the child who is dressed in a white baptismal garment.

Such scenes fill the mind's eye of many parental couples and perhaps even most churchgoing couples when they think of baptism. But veteran ministers who baptize know they are often looking at a more complex scene. For example, in some cases they may be baptizing the child of a single mother who chose to be fertilized *in vitro* because her "clock" was running out and she wanted a child of her own but had no spouse in view—or even no taste for having a spouse in view. Let the churches divide over the political and ethical issues in that case, or where, as in some parishes, a gay couple will be the presenting parents.

In some cases the counseling minister will be aware that the baby's father has died, or that in the nine months since conception of the child, the parents divorced and the father stands in the distance, if he is present at all. If he is attending, it is not likely that he can join in to make a commitment for the child's Christian upbringing, as he might if the couple were together and working in harmony.

Whoever writes to you parents today, as I am doing, also has to take cultural differences into consideration. Ethnicity plays its role in adding social issues. Each set of people in the "pentagon" of Christian peoples in America is made up of innumerable subdivisions, and each "does" baptism differently. Native-, Asian-,

African-, Latino/a-, and Euro-American Christians often have different concepts of family culture and do not pay all that much attention to the ways churches in other cultural groups practice these ceremonies of church and family. As Christians, they all use water and the Word of Jesus associated with baptism in the gospels, but similarities end there. In some cultures the parents are surrounded by uncles and aunts and undefined relatives. In some Euro-American cultures the presenting couple may have few roots and bonds, and cannot attract an extended family to the event. Some baptisms are quiet and solemn, while others erupt in celebratory noise. In some the mother is "all" while in others the father is a true partner. Parents are sometimes represented by a sole mother, whose man, perhaps an abuser, walked or was pushed away from her. Sometimes parents are incompetent, thoughtless, and improvident, and "never get around" to things of the spirit, so an aunt or uncle convinces the parents that she or he will take charge spiritually. Such a person will in effect act as the spiritual role of parent, leaving the birth mother and her man in the shadows.

We keep all these alternatives in mind but, for the sake of focus and clarity, we will describe the kind of parental situation that sounds standard and will evoke recall from many parents beside yourself. Everyone else may lean over your shoulder, read what applies to them, and use their imagination to think beyond that small circuit.

Dear parents: you are in the most dangerous situation of all. You were blessed with a child, and you take parental roles seriously. You prayed for this child, arranged for new expenses, went shopping, readied a nursery, sent birth announcements by the hundreds, and are seriously ready to assume the demands of care, with the hoped-for help of others.

Early in this book we spoke of baptizing as doing something dangerous. The infant is not aware of things, so the perilous context belongs to the parents, be they biological or adoptive. It is dangerous because, with the promises you make, you are committing yourself to the teaching and nurturing of Christian faith. The baptismal service does not allow for any leeway or anticipate any exceptions. You say "I do" or "I will," promising care that commits you to a no-matter-what circumstance. Of course, at such moments as this, you trust in and rely on the promises of God. They are the only feature of life in the future in which you can have confidence.

When it comes to planning for the circumstances of the future, however, it is all risk. The mother here gave birth in the physical sense to this child. The baby came forced and then freed out of her womb. She was there—and, one hopes, so was the father—when the medics did all the little rituals that contribute to the child's physical well-being. And then, and now . . . ?

Earlier we referred to a story that merits revisiting, an event in John's gospel in which Nicodemus, a ruler of the Jews, sneaked into Jesus' presence one night, afraid of being seen, and evidencing the courage it took to consult the often-despised Jesus. His question is old, but serious parents are still asking it, also for the baby: "What must I do to be saved?" As the Fourth Gospel tells it, Jesus does not directly answer the question, but takes the topic in a different direction. He tells Nicodemus that he must be born "again" or "from above" if he is to have any part in the kingdom. The natural question came to Nicodemus: "How can that be? Must I reverse my trail and climb back into my mother's womb?"

Jesus' answer may or may not bear directly on baptism, but it certainly does indirectly. Nicodemus must be born "from above" and be born "of water and the spirit." While not trying to settle old arguments among translators and commentators, we can say that whether or not John's gospel understands Jesus as having baptism in mind, the church has connected his words with baptism and the quest for salvation. So it is that many Christians speak of being "born again," perhaps through their adult baptism, or perhaps by an act of will, one of "owning Christ" and being owned by Christ. For our purposes, it is enough to picture baptism as related to this birth "from above."

Today's parents need not come at night, or secretly (unless figuratively, if they are sneaking the child to be baptized past hostile relatives on either or both sides of the family) but they are more likely to be bold, feeling themselves smiled on in the culture. You may be such. You may have many things on your minds, including concern for the proper vintage of champagne, the availability of the church on the day you would choose, along with some wardrobe choices for the child. You will have to think of the travel expenses of relatives who come, some medical bills still due, and nursery furnishing expenses.

For all that, you are to focus on God's gift to you, and your response. Odds are good that you will concentrate on the words addressed to parents in the ceremony. Typically, the minister will turn to you and "the sponsors," and ask, *called by the Holy Spirit, trusting in the grace and love of God, do you desire (child's name) to be baptized into Christ?*" You will answer, "*I do.*" Soon the "parents and sponsors" get in deeper when, speaking for the child, they "*renounce the devil and all the forces that defy God . . . [and] the powers of this world that rebel against God . . . [and] the ways of sin that draw you from God.*" Three times you, speaking for the child, will say you renounce them.

Sometimes at this point I almost want to shout out, "Do you know what you are doing? Do you know what you are saying? You are kicking over the ordinary props on which our lives are built. When this is finished, you have nothing left in front of you except the God who would block your path or guide your path. Are you ready for that?"

Fortunately, the creed then comes along, and you can join "the faith" and the faithful of the church in finding something on which to lean and which to borrow. Then the baptizer and the baptizee occupy the center of the scene and we do not hear of the parents at the crucial moment. After the baptism "the sponsor of a young child" may step forward to receive a candle and the parents recede further. The child, now a child of God, born from above as well as from the mother's womb, is handed back to you. Soon you will walk out into a world in which the renounced forces are there to smile on you and beguile you. You will need all the help you can get.

Perhaps there will be a couple of hours while cameras can still capture something of the day as relatives and friends dine, gifts get opened by the parents and sponsors, once again acting on and for the child. People will leave, night will fall, and it will dawn on you that you were overwhelmed by the grace showered on your child and now you get to pray for some for yourselves!

Users of baptism especially know, or learn, that with the dawn of the next day, as they make the sign of the cross, turn to God in repentance, and receive the grace to walk in newness of life, they are involving their children. In a couple of years, in the bedroom or nursery or children's book library, they will be able to read to them, introducing them to aspects of the faith appropriate to their age. In many congregations there is encouragement for children to learn the disciplines of silence and worship with their parents—it can be done! They can come forward for a children's sermon and then trot off to church school. As years pass they can go to church camp, and at annual recalls of their baptismal day they might gain a deeper understanding of what happened to them on their baptismal day. Most of this nurturing can go on without a parent or parents, but parents are really key to it all. You parents need daily renewal if you are to assist your child in experiencing the newness of life and knowing its source.

A conversation with a child's godparents

Parents and grandparents ought to care about what is said to these responsible sponsors, be they relatives or not. Since more parents survive through the child's growing years than they did centuries ago, some of the duties of the godparents are treated less urgently today than they were in previous generations. Yet in a "you never know when" spirit, godparents or sponsors, as always, need to have their duties spelled out and the resources that will back them up reinforced. The sponsors again represent everyone present at a baptism or who care for the child and baptized children. So we listen in:

Dear sponsors or godparents:

The circle of those involved in a baptism now grows. We have spoken to and about adults and children. In the case of infant baptism, some adult believers, who may be called "sponsors" or "godparents," are on the scene to witness, speak for the child, and commit themselves to the spiritual care of the child. Since you are among these, let me address this specifically to you.

If you were a sponsor years ago and have been neglectful, this is a good time to revisit your pledge and begin to live up to it. In what follows, let me address you as godparents in the past who might want to make up for lost time, as well as new godparents right now, or godparents-to-be. If I go on a bit long on this easily overlooked subject, I do so because if we are to put baptism to use, we will need all the help we can get. The infant is unaware of what is going on, and parents have a full agenda, so you are the ones who can concentrate on what is going on. When parents invite you to be a godparent, they are honoring you, signaling something to their child, and investing in your future role.

Unlucky you, godparents. There is not a line of scripture commanding, authorizing, or blessing your role as such. Having sponsors is a human custom, not part of the sacrament. It is an invention to help make the ceremony more meaningful and to assure that there will be aids for the child when it comes to the use of baptism. Still, this role needs accent as seldom before, and godparents have to be chosen with special care today. I know that what I am writing here can go against the grain of the culture. A parent or parents of a child want a baptism to be "done," so they want to do it right—which includes naming godparents. The people they choose ordinarily are people they admire; who would blight their child by putting a bad role model before him? You godparents are chosen, and as the children grow they are to learn who their godparents are and why they were chosen. If the choice is made simply to seal old friendships or to pay old emotional debts or to have a good time at a baptismal dinner, it shows that the whole idea of godparenting has not penetrated the consciousness of parents and other caregivers.

Certainly the first criterion in your choice was that you are yourself a baptized Christian. If you are church-shopping or have been unwilling to confirm your baptism into the body of Christ which is the church, you are not likely to be moved or able to pass on to someone else the reasons for living the full life in Christ.

I know that this concept of godparenting can create some emotional problems—especially when some are *not* chosen. Hurt feelings are many: "I stood up for their wedding, and now they don't remember me." "I guess I am not good enough for these old friends, who have grown clubby and distant since they 'got religion' and became active in church." "It should be my turn to show up in support of that family. The fact that I am not a believer should not count; baptism, after all, is between God and the child."

There are thousands of ways to pass out favors or pay old debts, but naming godparents is not a good place to start. You read the job description for what a godparent or sponsor takes on at the baptismal service. It all goes with the territory. Whether there are two or three is up to those who bring the child to baptism. Often the godparents are relatives; sometimes it is good to draw beyond the circle of relatives to add riches and imagination to the adventure of living the life of the baptized. If you think about it, you will also likely conclude that it is ordinarily not best to choose great-grandparents to be godparents, since people in their age group are not likely to be around long enough to see the baptized child through enough stages and courses of life. If the receiving community or congregation is large enough to have classes for parents of a child to be baptized, it is profitable for all if godparents also attend and learn more of what it is all about.

There are few honors or responsibilities higher than those that go with godparenting. Parents and other family members are, in effect, pinning a badge of honor or handing out a certificate of achievement and commitment to you when you are chosen. If we believe that baptism has eternal consequences, then we have to believe that being a godparent relates to those eternal prospects. While you godparents are not to be busybodies or snoops, and while you have certain bounds of etiquette to follow, yet, if you were well chosen and have good relations with the parents, you will find ways to stand by with counsel and offers of aid.

The task of godparenting begins on the day of baptism, when you make promises. In many traditions, including those that have been influenced by Martin Luther, the faith of the godparent is itself a sign and signal of the fact that the family of God's children are involved with the destiny of *this* child. Godparents are, in a way, agents of the parents to the congregation and agents of the congregation to the parents.

There are many ways to fulfill your roles. Among these are praying for the child and worshiping with the parents and annually sending greeting cards or giving gifts on the anniversaries of baptism. Sometimes children will more readily accompany godparents, who are giving of their time, than their own parents to faith-building events and opportunities. And sometimes when parents are neglectful of their duties and privileges when it comes to worship, godparents can offer to buzz by to pick the child up, take her along, and make an event of the day. Pizza after church is not a sacrament, but it can make a holy act more attractive.

In our global society, effectively fulfilling the duties of godparents can become difficult. The godparents may be transferred to Singapore while the child lives in Albany. The child may have parents in the military or international business who are regularly transferred. In a time when transportation is easy and e-mail and cell phones are pervasive, it is easier to stay in touch across the miles and the years, but it takes considerable intentionality. When a child and his godparents live at great distance from each other, some Christian communities will appoint local surrogate godparents who can do all that godparents do except recall having been witnesses at the baptism.

Sometimes you godparents are chosen to take over if parents become incapacitated or alienated or if they die. Provident parents picture whom they admire, people who could take over child care, so they often name godparents as legal guardians. When such designating is possible it makes good sense, but one does not choose godparents on the basis of their financial means and savvy or business finesse. There are other ways to appoint guardians for a child. Still, godparenting and guardianship can go together well and together they symbolize "all-purpose" care and concern.

As a child grows, godparents as mentors can also be fun-loving companions. Many a grown child describes with delight godparent visits, overnights, summer vacations, reading times, and other means by which adults reinforce the life of faith. There are so many assaults on faith and baptism that one can no longer take godparenting for granted. To be a godly godparent is to be a caregiver who has the best of intentions *and* who acts on them.

The gospel for the baptizer

In most cases, a minister of the gospel will be the one who baptizes. In large congregations, pastors will be baptizing infants more weeks than not, a privilege that goes with their office—and a perilous responsibility because it can produce unthinking ritualists. Those "reverends" who celebrate their own baptism daily are most likely to stand in awe of the act in which they get to participate. It should be of interest to the majority of Christians, often called laypeople, to picture what goes with being a minister who is charged with baptizing or, to put it another way, gets to baptize.

Dear ministers or others who are appointed to see to it that baptism occurs responsibly:

If the families of infants who are being baptized read what I write to you, they will have a better sense of the terror and joy that go with the office of baptizing. If an adult preparing for baptism is reading it, she will recognize that you are not just fill-ing a ceremonial role.

In the case of adult baptisms, odds are that you the bap-tizer have spent some evenings with a class of people who are inquiring, addressing their issues of faith and possible place on the church rolls. You may have spent long hours in the inquirer's home, taking up issues the family brings up. "Dad" had resisted pleas that he examine faith commitments, but now he wants to take on the responsibility of a Christian parent, and he wants to be in Christian company by being baptized. He had almost more questions than you had answers, but when it was over you told yourself that preparation for baptism and counseling about its consequences are among the most rewarding features of your ministry. The press does not know this, and the TV cameras are nowhere to be seen. But you are there, and the one to be baptized knows the role you are playing as God's deputy.

Why then speak, once more, of the gentle scene that follows as occurring at the edge of terror? Using a phrase like that can seem a bit melodramatic. But it is not. Terror might well be expe-rienced because, as a participant in this profound transaction between God and the human, you are aware of your fallibility, of what you do not know, of what you failed to impart imagina-tively. You reflect on your shortcomings when standing in the front of the pre-baptism class. You remember times when the workload led you to become impatient and you risked having the candidate for baptism lose patience and, perhaps, disappear. Maybe you did not present with sufficient seriousness the call of God, the demands of the divine law. Worse, you may not have done any kind of justice to the good news that lures people to God, to faith, to baptism. Worse still, when this class is over, you will before long have to get ready for another—by which time you may discover that some of those you have already baptized have already turned cold, gotten distracted, or walked away.

So there are reasons for terror. You, however, did not accept the call to visit, teach, and baptize in order to become a psychological mess because you are aware of the distance between what you are and what, under God, you wish to be. We won't hurry past that point, because we hope that those looking over your shoulder, which is what reading these pages amounts to, will have the point deeply stamped in their minds: God trusts God's message to the deafness of mortals, using the half-tied tongues of fallible people. Despite your fallibilities, in the mystery of God you are an agent of God.

On the other hand, lingering on all this for too long could create the impression that everything depends on you just because at the moment you are standing in as a deputy for Christ, gifted to do something great. And there is the danger that the fact that you might baptize often in the space of a year or, certainly, through a lifetime, might lead you to treat the miracle of your call casually.

I have heard of a great violinist who, backstage before he went before the orchestra and the audience, paced and fretted. He even smoked a cigarette up to the last minute. Someone asked, "Why are you nervous? You have done this hundreds of times before!" He answered, pointing to the curtain that for only one more moment would protect him, "Not before *this* audience!" The use of our gifts should never be taken casually.

If you, the baptizer, are also a preacher, we hope you still feel the nervousness that comes with responsibility before you open your mouth. And now, with the baptism coming up, we hope you are awed, and perhaps a bit nervous, thinking that today a child of God, eight days or eighty years old, is being born—and you are privileged to be part of the event. God's promises are sure; God will not mess anything up. But you, through a casual or routine approach, might well fail in communicating a sense of the specialness of this occasion and all that it implies.

"Come off it!" I can almost hear you say. "Don't be histrionic. You are just writing a chapter of counsel to someone who is likely to walk from a sacristy into a sanctuary, open a book, read from it, and apply water to a child or an adult. When it is done, the baptized person's days will continue, and so will those of the baptizer. What is more, the one who does the baptizing is not the real baptizer but only the momentary agent of the 'Father and of the Son and of the Holy Spirit.'"

And that, of course is true—the real baptizer is God and the one who does the baptizing is a sinner, someone who might personally be of weak faith or even—though we hope not!—of no faith. So long as this person invokes the divine Trinity, proclaims the Word, and applies water in the name of the triune God, baptism has been effected. If it were any other way, what comfort could the adult who presents herself or the parents who bring a child ever find? We hope that faith, which is a gift, will be nurtured in the one baptized and in those who witness the baptism by the character of the baptizer, but the gift comes no matter who is the human agent.

And the human agent need not be a pastor or priest. This is the place to remind readers that, even though an ordained cleric is often the one who takes people down to the river or over to the font, any Christian can do the baptizing in an emergency. On occasion, for instance, the baptizer may be a nurse in the NIC unit, where the neonatal human needs intensive care supported by intensive prayer. On other occasions the baptizer may be not a chaplain but a chaplain's assistant or an informed nonprofessional lay person. While those are extraordinary circumstances, one holds them in mind to keep the focus on the water and the Word and the faith that is associated with baptism.

Interestingly, in a great Reformation-era painting by Lucas Cranach, one that illustrates baptism in Luther's time, the one who does the baptizing is scholar Philip Melanchthon, one of the few in Luther's inner circle who was never ordained. The point is clear: the baptizer's credentials are not what matter for baptism to be effective.

Having said all that, it is time to return to the scene of most baptisms, especially of children, in our day. The thrill of being someone who baptizes is also associated with the call for you to follow through after baptism. This may mean sending regular messages from the pulpit, in class, or in private counsel, words that will help teach people how to use their baptism. Such messages will remind those who hear them to make use of the other sacrament, the Lord's Supper, often called the Eucharist, and to be regular in attendance at worship where Christ is present with two or three or three hundred gathered in his name.

Following through for you who baptize might mean showing the courage to admonish when admonition is in order. Admonition is not an often-used term or practice in most Christian circles. Yet it is counseled and given as a charge to Christian leaders in the New Testament. To admonish does not mean to be a spy or scold, a busybody who finds it important to disapprove of everything that neglectful parents of a baptized child do or do not do. It does, however, mean entering with "grace" into the lives of people commended to your care. It also means speaking humbly but firmly in conscience to help the baptized person remain true to the covenant spoken of on the baptismal day.

The user of baptism should be seen as someone hungry for the good news, eager to gain spiritual weaponry against temptation, and alert to the promise of God, which is not likely to be heard in the general culture. Here you who baptize can know the greatest joy: to help the baptized affirm their baptism, return to the promises, be lifted out of doubt or near-despair, and be given a vision of a life that pleases God and helps the neighbor.

Finally, it is fair to expect that from time to time you who baptize will be a user of baptism! It is fair to expect you to focus on the uses of baptism in your retreats, your private devotion and study, and your conversation. Baptism is both a "done deal" *and* a covenant into which one—including those who baptize—grows lifelong, with the help of others. It is a great calling and responsibility both to baptize others and to use baptism yourself.

Words for the community that receives the baptized

As you will see when you read this section, if you are a Christian who attempts to live the graced and disciplined life of a child of God and are in a context where new children or adults receive baptism, you are involved. So let's get right to the point.

Dear disciples of Christ who are formed as a community or congregation where baptisms occur:

Worshiping with a group of Christians on the occasion of a baptism is in its own way a dangerous act, graced as it is and rich with the promises of God in faith. Here is why: just before the profession of faith in the form of the Apostles' Creed, in most baptismal orders of service, "the presiding minister addresses the assembly":

> *People of God, do you promise to support [John and Mary]*
> *and pray for them in their new life in Christ?*
> **We do.** (ELW, 228)

That bold-faced type in the service book can be a bold-faced lie, and it is hazardous to lie before God. Better to have rolled over in bed and stayed home than to have promised to do something as important as "to support" someone who is going to be baptized by mouthing those two words without being thoughtful or without meaning them. If you are a casual visitor to a baptizing congregation, someone who just dropped in or is looking over both the place and the faith, you can rationalize your choice to remain silent. You are not a part of the assembly in the deepest sense of commitment, and, in effect, "the presiding minister" has not asked you anything. You are for the moment home free. But if you should become baptized, or as one already baptized become part of the assembly, then you are being put on notice as to the startling thing you will be asked to do: support. And pray.

Suppose you *are* a confirmed and committed member of the assembly, and the baptized person is an adult. You are "just anybody," and at the font is a 250-pound football player, an opera singer, a CEO of a corporation, or a candidate for public office. Let's say that one or another of these is marrying a member of the congregation. As love grew between the bride- and groom-to-be, so did curiosity about what "makes the other tick." That curiosity took the form of his or her following through by joining an inquirer's class. The focus of the gospel and the work of the Holy Spirit led the inquirer to desire baptism and become a part of the Christian family. Would such a person be asking for support? From you?

Quarterbacks work with the support cast of the team. Divas count on support by orchestra and chorus and prompters. CEOs, even if they are self-made women or men, are backed by support staffs. Politicians ask for your support. All those forms of support are easily explained and utilized. As for "support" in the Christian life, however, we have to ask: Who requested fellow Christians to provide it? Those in the pew may not even know the name of the one being baptized and, in the case of large and mobile congregations, may never see that person again. It seems like idle chatter to say that these congregants will support the one being baptized. They may not even remember the name later in the same day, and they will pray only in the prayer during the baptismal service or generically, as when people pray for "the whole people of God."

Chances are, while they expect friendly greetings, the newly baptized may not want their privacy invaded, and so it may be hard for the congregation to learn what kind of support might be needed. Newcomers may be very shy and even nervous about greeting someone they do not know well, or know at all. The kind of support the baptized need is likely to relate to intimate aspects of their faith, their temptations, the condition of their soul, their coping with grief, or their jumping up in joy when good news comes or good things happen. The "support" of someone who is a stranger or a remote congregational acquaintance might seem to offer little and might even irritate.

Some untrained people are gifted at discerning the mindset of others, but they usually do not exercise this gift until they know another person well enough to win their confidence to the point that they are willing to unburden themselves of their problems and needs or discuss the situation of their souls. Such interactions between the baptized may not happen often, but they do happen, and when they do, life-changing results can occur.

The interaction might occur during a break in a game, during long delays at a sporting event, over a cup of coffee in a restaurant or in the church's fellowship hall after worship. It might begin when a new friend reads worry or dismay on the face of another, and learns that he has just been diagnosed with a serious illness or has lost his job. Or the worry might be over a son or daughter who has left for college; the nest is empty, and the parents have to redefine themselves. Perhaps someone is troubled over—and needs to talk about—the burden of child rearing. When confidence is deep, one might even describe a temptation that is hard to resist, something connected with life at the office, in the faculty club, or at a homeless shelter. The reader of the face of someone troubled does not lunge in and brashly offer advice or pronounce judgment, but unanxiously waits, builds the relationship, and listens carefully when the moment of confidence and unburdening arrives.

So what does it mean to "support" the child being baptized or the adult who becomes a new member of the assembly? Mentioning prayer sounds perfunctory, but there are ways to make it vivid, exacting, and demanding—and it can be the occasion for support. Any member of the assembly might find herself sitting down for a conversation with someone else and discovering that prayer is in order—and then follow up by praying.

Prayer is also a climactic feature in Christian worship, so each Sunday we hear:

With the whole people of God in Christ Jesus, let us pray
for the church, those in need, and all of God's creation.

That bidding poises you to "support." The baptized person is of "the church," is "in need," and is aware of being part of "God's creation." When the prayers are said, congregants sometimes are invited to name people for whom to pray. What if they did more than mumble under their breath the name and situation of people in a war zone, in government, or in hospitals—what if they lifted up before God the name of someone at whose baptism they have been present? General prayers then do not remain general or generic. They become particular, and if worshipers believe that prayer is not pointless, then this praying has a point, and it *will* lead to support—it *is* support. Whenever our prayer asks that a fellow believer accept each new day as an opportunity to realize what it is to be forgiven and an opportunity to learn why not to worry about the future, we are providing the support promised in the baptismal service.

Members of congregations who live in the same place for a number of years and who remain in the congregation where a particular infant has been baptized can show support in many ways. This can be done virtually anonymously by helping provide for nursery and church school or summer camp opportunities designed to aid in a young person's "growth in grace." There are so many ways the people who say, "**We do,**" when asked if they will support the baptized, can provide such support.

In many orders of worship for baptizing there is one more way in which the supporting and praying congregation gets involved:

The ministers and the baptismal group face the assembly. A representative of the congregation leads the assembly in the welcome.

> **We welcome you into the body of Christ and into the mission we share: join us in giving thanks and praise to God and bearing God's creative and redeeming word to all the world.** (ELW, 231)

Then everything returns to normal: "Those who have gathered at the font may return to their places." There is an additional option: "An acclamation, psalm, or hymn may be sung." After all this, a typical line in the book will say, "the service continues . . ." but, in the larger sense of the term, "the service" outside the place of worship continues through life.

In a week, the assembly will regather and more new "belongers to Christ" may emerge in the place we have been imagining, or in hundreds of thousands of other places where millions of the people who "belong to Christ" respond to his command to "Go . . . and baptize."

After this exercise with a service book and hymnbook, it is time to close it and move on to some questions and elaborations that we can offer and address with the aid of other books that Christians share. Each communion offers some version or other of a "theology of the church," which includes a focus on what was here called "the assembly" or could be "the congregation" and in this section's title is "the community." There are likely to be some differences among them, depending upon how ancient is the theology, or what is the context. The "community" that gathers under a thatched roof in a new Pentecostal congregation in Kenya, under the vault of a cathedral in Brazil, or in a plain white country church in the Dakotas, will picture community in a variety of diverse ways. Those whose accent is either Protestant or Catholic or Orthodox will approach the common life of those baptized in Christ in a variety of distinctive ways. Some of these ways are grounded in differences that can be enduring and perplexing, but most of these do not affect our present point, which calls us to say to the adult or child just baptized, "We welcome you into the body of Christ and into the mission we share."

Those words might still be echoing in a baptismal chapel when the question comes: By what right do "we" welcome someone into the body of Christ? Only the Holy Spirit can do that, since baptism is an activity by humans but "in the name of the Father and of the Son and of the Holy Spirit." The God of grace is the one who invites, welcomes, and sends forth believers. Yet if that word of welcome is to make any sense at all, and does not represent mere arrogance, it has to have some backing in the Word of God. Think of it this way: the "welcomers" are, at that moment and for this purpose, deputies of God the Father, vicars of God the Son, and representatives of God the Holy Spirit. The divine Trinity is present to assure that through the humble element of water and the raspy voice of a minister, baptism is not a mere ceremony, a ritual one "goes through" for old times' or a new family's sake. God *is* present. Something *is* happening. That is why a congregation making a commitment to the baptized has to plead for help and be sufficiently sure of itself to step into this stand-in role. They are continuing to bid for discipleship in Jesus' name.

In his great book *The Cost of Discipleship,* Dietrich Bonhoeffer put it more dramatically, but truly, than most of those who form a congregation for baptism might: "When Jesus Christ calls a person, he calls him to die." For Bonhoeffer and millions before him, all the way back to disciples like Stephen and James the apostles, this call has been literal. Its potential for sacrifice endures. This is hard to grasp, for example, in a suburban congregation in an affluent society and under a government currently regarded as benign. This call through baptism has often reached people who are apparently well-off and secure, but whose fortunes change with war, ruthless governments, and new policies by regimes.

Do we then say, "We welcome you into the body of Christ and into the fellowship of suffering, which may mean your death?" Are "we" co-executioners? Of course, posing it that way is for most Christians most of the time far too dramatic. Yet "we," in the name of an infant or at the side of an adult who is speaking for himself, have in baptism "renounced" the devil, the forces that defy God, and the ways of sin that draw us from God. From the time the gospels were written until now, we know that what is represented by the devil, the forces, and the ways of sin live on. The decisive victory over them was won by Jesus Christ in the resurrection, but until the coming again of Christ, declare the creeds and congregations, these enemies will live on, defeated but not disappeared. So the baptized person cannot face them alone. "We" welcome that person.

Who are "we"? Some of us resent it when writers on magazine covers or in headlines speak for us, as in, "Why We Are Growing More Obese" or "Why We Are Not Hip-Hop Fans" or "Why We Support the War." Who asked "you," the writers and editors and publishers, to speak for us? So it is important for us to be as precise as possible in defining the "we." It is for that purpose that we look at the Large Catechism of Martin Luther. Right off, we read, "First we take up baptism, through which we are initially received into the Christian community." Lest there be any doubt: "To be baptized in God's name is to be baptized not by human beings but by God himself. Although it is performed by human hands, it is nevertheless truly God's own act." A couple of pages later the word about the community reappears, when readers are asked to tell "why God ordained precisely this sign and external ceremony for the sacrament by which we are first received into the Christian community."

The reference is to the Apostles' Creed: "I believe in the Holy Spirit, one holy Christian church, the community of saints." "Community" gets a one-line footnote in the favored English translation: "German: *Gemeine*." The German is sometimes translated as "congregation" or "assembly." Continuing, the Holy Spirit makes us holy "through the Christian church," which means "in the first place, he has a unique community in the world, which is the mother that begets and bears every Christian through the Word of God. . . ." In short, in a profound sense, we are not Christian because we choose to be Christian, we are not members of the church because we choose to be members of the church. The Holy Spirit has called us and placed us in the "lap of the church." An audacious paragraph soon follows:

> I believe that there is on earth a holy little flock and community of pure saints under one head, Christ. It is called together by the Holy Spirit in one faith, mind, and understanding; it possesses a variety of gifts, and yet is united in love without sect or schism. Of this community I also am a part and member, a participant and co-partner in all the blessings it poses. I was brought into it by the Holy Spirit and incorporated into it through the fact that I have heard and still hear God's Word, which is the beginning point for entering it. Before we had come into this community, we were entirely of the devil, knowing nothing of God and of Christ. The Holy Spirit will remain with the holy community or Christian people until the Last Day. . . . Further we believe that in this Christian community we have the forgiveness of sins, which takes place though the holy sacrament and absolution as well as through all the comforting words of the entire gospel. (BOC, 427-438)

In words that find parallels in other traditions, that says something of who "we" are who welcome the newly baptized.

The stress on the community, congregation, assembly, parish, or church (as in local or worldwide) is so strong because baptism is not a personal or private or family drama, but an act of the Holy Spirit through the whole church, represented in its local embodiment. The communal form needs emphasis in a time when many stress their individualism; their isolation from Christian community; their rage against, distance from, or rebellion against the community usually described as "organized religion" or "the institutional church." As a check against such individualism, we might well ponder Dietrich Bonhoeffer's shocking assertion that "Christ exists *as* community," and there is no other place or way in the tradition of the apostles to "have" Christ. Christ is present in the preached and sung word and in the sacraments: "This is my body. This is my blood." Christ is present in "the other," who needs and offers care. Christ is present "where two or three are gathered in his name" to connect each individual community to the whole Christian community.

This community, as mentioned, does not baptize, but receives the baptized. To make good on the pledge to "support" the newly baptized is to help assure that she is brought up or, for adults, constantly grows within, the community for the sake of the world. Baptism is a social or community activity that demands the follow-through of a community.

A local congregation can do much to help baptized Christians realize the promise of their baptism. Every baptism is an occasion for teaching and doing some reminding. Preachers alert to the rich promise of baptism include reference to it in many homilies. That is not hard to do, because almost all the gospel readings on which sermons and homilies are based depict the benefits that we associate with baptism. Counselors also use the "dailiness" of baptism, to which thoughtful Christians turn when they make the sign of the cross in the morning and in the evening. With that in mind and heart, and with God's action, the past is left behind and the future is not a simple occasion for worry: Christ forgave the sins of yesterday and promises to be with the believer today and tomorrow.

Further reminders are present when, following an increasing practice, churches relocate the baptismal font or pool near the entrance of the church or, in the case of new churches, often arrange for a large font and pool in which there is flowing water. Some worshipers, as they pass it, dip their fingers and make the sign of the cross upon themselves. No one pretends that this "simple water" and its use make up a sacrament, but many find that they do serve as prompts for memory and hope.

In many congregations on certain days, worshipers especially recall and celebrate their baptism with a ceremony called *asperges*, meaning "sprinkling with water." In Catholicism the water is blessed and called "holy water." In most other traditions this sprinkling is with "simple water," but it is a water of remembrance. The ministers walk through a congregation, dipping a branch into water and sprinkling the congregation. This is done especially in the Easter season, following the opening words of Psalm 51. In a cool church one will hear the children present responding to the chill of the sprinkling, and may see adults half-ducking as they await the cold splash. No one is pretending that anything miraculous is going on, or that this sprinkling is a sacrament. Not commanded by God and exercised without specific promises, it belongs to the whole flow of Christian life in congregation or community, and is a *reminder* of the benefits of baptism—a reminder to the sprinkled and blessed to put their baptism once more to use.

We can leave this user's guide at this point, where the baptized keep on receiving the gifts and benefits of baptism with the awareness that now they get to pass them on to others. These others are part of a family of more than two billion people called by the Holy Spirit, blessed by the Father, and embodying the gifts of the divine Son. They have a word to use when the enemies of faith come: "I am baptized! I am marked with the cross of Christ forever!" And a word from the gospel still impels them: "Go therefore . . . make disciples . . . baptizing . . . and teaching them. . . ." And when they do just that, they are demonstrating one more way of using baptism.

Questions for Reflection
and Discussion

Chapter 1. Using the Baptismal Sign of the Cross—Daily

1. Do you presently use the sign of the cross as a means of recalling the promises, gifts, commitments, and obligations of baptism? If so, at what times do you follow this practice? In what ways does this practice assist your growth in faith and faithfulness? If not, why not give it a conscientious try?

2. What other practices might one do as a means of recalling the promises, gifts, commitments, and obligations of baptism?

3. Why might the daily remembrance of baptism enable you to "go to your work joyfully" in the morning and "go to sleep quickly and cheerfully" at night?

4. Does it make sense to you to say that repentance is a joyful experience? Why or why not?

Chapter 2. The Dangerous Grace of Baptizing

1. According to baptismal liturgies, baptism joins us to "God's mission in the world" and calls us to "grow in faith, love, and obedience to the will of God." Does this strike you as dangerous language? Why or why not?

2. Is your baptism, with its promises, gifts, commitments, and obligations, a call to live a "risky" life that might lead to persecution and suffering? Explain.

3. How would you describe the "danger" that accompanies baptism for (1) the one baptized, (2) those who present him or her for baptism, and (3) the community of faith where the baptism takes place?

4. What do you think is essential in baptism, and what are merely externals and, therefore, unessential? Why?

Chapter 3. Using the Faith Connected with Baptism

1. How would you describe the relationship between baptism and repentance? Between baptism and forgiveness of sins?

2. How do the commands from Matthew 28—*go, baptize, teach*—both describe and guide the church's mission?

3. We have stressed the role and importance of baptism in the early church. Do you think that baptism is taken with the same seriousness in our time and culture as it was back then? Why or why not?

4. What might be done to strengthen the role and use of baptism in the modern church?

Chapter 4. The Useful Gifts and Benefits of Baptism

1. What experiences have you had (or could you imagine having) that might "dash" the "expectations and hopes" that are associated with baptism?
2. What signs of the Spirit's presence and power are you aware of in your life? In the lives of others?
3. Would you say that you do or do not pay the "cost of discipleship" in your life of faith? Explain.
4. Skim through this chapter again and make a list of all the "gifts and benefits of baptism" that you find. Reflect on each of these gifts and benefits. What are some concrete ways you can "use" each of them each day as you continue "to grow in faith, love, and obedience to the will of God?"

Chapter 5. Water Alone Is Useless in Baptism

1. What are the qualities of water that make it the perfect element for baptism?
2. How might the various ways you use water throughout the day be used to remind you to return to your baptism and its gifts and promises?
3. Trying to explain *how* the Word is *with* and *alongside* and *in* the water leads inevitably to *mystery*. It has been said that mysteries are not meant to be explained, they are meant to be lived in. Are you comfortable with mystery? Why or why not? What does it mean to you to "live in" the mystery of the connection between Word and water in baptism?

4. What differences (if any) do you see in faith as *trust* and faith as mere belief? How might faith *as trust in God's Word in baptism* both challenge and change daily life?

Chapter 6. The Significance of Baptism with Water

1. What does it mean to you to "consider yourself dead to sin and alive to God in Christ Jesus" (Romans 6:11) through your baptism and your daily return to it?
2. In what ways is "daily sorrow for sin" expressed in your life?
3. Do you experience yourself as coming forth each day as a new person? Why or why not?
4. In what ways does the fact that you have been both buried with Christ and raised to newness of life impact the decisions you make in getting from morning to night?

Chapter 7. The Dangers and Rewards of Infant Baptism

1. What does it mean to take baptism for granted in the case of infant baptism?
2. In what ways is it true that taking baptism for granted or being indifferent to it can contribute to "spiritual death"?
3. In what ways might a daily return to baptism help one to avoid other causes of a "descent toward spiritual death"?
4. Does it matter to you that one cannot make a strong biblical case for or against infant baptism? Why or why not?

Chapter 8. Baptism and Faith—Faith and Baptism

1. After reading this chapter, how do you understand the relationship between faith and baptism?
2. There are two branches in Christianity with respect to baptism—those who baptize infants (and previously unbaptized adults) and those who only baptize adult believers. What differences might you expect to find in the faith, life, and religious practice of believers in these different branches? Why?
3. How does infant baptism "throw light on all biblical teaching and church practice as these relate to faith"?
4. Infant baptism witnesses to our helplessness and dependence before God. How might a clear awareness of such helplessness and dependence positively influence a believer's life of faith and spiritual growth?

Chapter 9. User's Guide to Baptism

1. Make a list of the ways believers can "use" baptism to help them navigate through life in our complex, chaotic, and often morally ambiguous world. Draw a circle around the "uses of baptism" you are already practicing. Draw a box around those you have neglected to practice but might begin to use now. What conclusions can you draw from this exercise?
2. What are the "advantages" of an adult baptism for (1) the one baptized, (2) those who present him or her for baptism, and (3) the community that witnesses the baptism?

3. What are the "advantages" of an infant baptism for (1) the one baptized, (2) those who present the child for baptism, and (3) the community that witnesses the baptism?

4. What are the obligations of support taken on by a community of faith that "welcomes" a newly baptized infant or adult into the church and the mission of God? Where can the community get help in carrying out its obligations?

Abbreviations

BOC *The Book of Concord: The Confessions of the Evangeli-cal Lutheran Church.* Ed. Robert Kolb and Timothy J. Wengert. Minneapolis: Fortress Press, 2000.

ELW *Evangelical Lutheran Worship.* Minneapolis: Augsburg Fortress, 2006.

LSC *Luther's Small Catechism.* Minneapolis: Augsburg Fortress, 2001.

PBH *Prayer Book and Hymnal: Containing the Book of Common Prayer and the Hymnal.* New York: The Church Hymnal Corporation, 1986.

Index of Topics

Accidie, 42
Adam and Eve, 55
adopt, adoption, 28, 124–125, 128, 132
adult baptism, 117, 134, 141, 161
Anabaptist, 27, 98
Anglican, 50
anointing, 22, 26, 45, 47–48, 122
Anomie, 42
apostolic tradition, 64
Aquinas, Thomas, 42
Asperges, 155
Auden, W. H., 57

baptism of desire, 72
Baptism, Eucharist, Ministry, 45
Baptist, 11, 23, 27–28, 31, 97–98
baptistry, 119
baptizee, 114–117, 119, 136
baptizer, 135, 140–144
Bonhoeffer, Dietrich, 41, 151, 154
Book of Common Prayer, 28, 50, 63
born again, 81, 84, 117, 134

Cantus firmus, 50, 51
catechism, Episcopal, 28, 51
catechisms, 28, 29, 34, 55, 60, 83–84, 103
catechumen, 29, 71, 114
Catholic, 28, 30, 64, 66, 71, 97–98, 150, 155
cheap grace, 53
circumcision, 35, 93–94
command, 5, 12, 29, 33, 47, 51, 57, 64, 74, 77–78, 86, 92, 97, 99–102, 107, 109, 127, 137, 150, 155, 158
communion, 21, 114, 117
community, 2, 14, 19, 21, 14, 16, 30, 34, 38–40, 50, 52, 62, 78–79, 82, 107, 118, 128, 129, 138, 145, 150, 152–156, 158, 161–162
congregation, 145–146, 149–155
Cornelius, 35
credobaptist, 28
Creed, 6, 20, 68, 70, 116, 135, 145, 152
Creed, Apostolic, 116
Creed, Nicene, 116

dailiness, 8, 154
danger (and baptism), 5–7, 11–13, 15–24, 26, 31, 40–41, 46, 53, 58, 71, 73, 76, 86, 89–93, 96, 99, 108, 115, 132–133, 142, 145, 158, 160
devil, 20, 26, 42, 50, 60–29, 134, 151–153
discipleship, 16, 41–3, 108, 158–59

early church, 40, 93, 158
ecumenical, 55, 98, 106
emergency baptism, 143
empowerment, 45–47
eternal salvation, 62, 67–68
Eucharist, 21, 45
Evangelical Lutheran Worship, 60
exorcism, 20, 64, 66

faith, 2, 13–15, 17–20, 25, 27, 31, 34, 38–39, 43, 45–47, 51–52, 58–59, 61, 63, 65–66, 68, 70, 72–73, 76–80, 82, 86, 88, 91–108, 110–111, 115–124, 133, 135, 139
Fides infantilis, 110
forgiveness, 2, 11, 28, 31, 29, 40, 50, 51–59, 64, 67, 69, 86, 127, 153, 158

Germany, East, 15
gifts and benefits, 2, 9, 14, 21, 41–45, 47, 49–53, 55, 57, 59–61, 63, 65, 67, 69, 70, 72, 74–76, 92, 135, 139, 142, 153, 156–159
godparents, 19–20, 26, 60, 64, 76, 91, 128, 129, 131, 136–140

Hebrew scriptures, 10, 30, 65
Hippolytus, 64
Holy Spirit, 3, 5, 10, 17, 19, 22, 24, 29, 33–35, 37, 40, 44–52, 67, 74, 76–78, 80, 99–104, 107, 109, 120, 134, 143, 146, 150–153, 155

Image of God, 56, 77
immersion, 23–24, 28, 30, 42, 74, 86–87
In vitro fertilization, 131
incorporation, 51
initiates, 62, 65–66
Israel, 22, 30–31, 35, 70, 72, 77

Jews, Judaism, 15, 35, 39, 55, 80–81, 126
John the Baptist, 11, 22, 31–34, 36–37, 43
justification, 28, 94

Large Catechism, 86, 99, 152
Latin, 25, 48, 83, 110
Lima document, 44
Limbo, 71
liturgy, 28, 60, 63–64, 70, 104, 158
Luther, Martin/Lutheran, 10, 25–26, 28–30, 33, 52, 60, 64–66, 69, 73, 75, 82–83, 97–98, 139, 144, 152
Luther: Between Man and the Devil, 65

magic, 1, 7, 9, 43, 58–59, 76, 96
Mark, 31
Mary, 14, 76, 80, 146
means of grace, 10
Melanchthon, Philip, 144
Mennonites, 27

minister, 10, 23, 60, 67, 108, 129–131, 134, 140, 145, 147, 151, 155
Missa catechumenorum, 114
Missa fidelium, 114
mystery, 44, 70, 128, 142, 159

Nicodemus, 81, 133
Noah, 22, 39, 70, 77

Oberman, Heiko, 65
old Adam, 83–84
original sin, 55–56
orthodox, 28–29, 56, 64, 97, 150

parents, 128–139, 141, 143–44, 148
pedobaptist, 28
Presentation, the, 13, 17, 19, 2, 31, 111
promise, 5, 9, 11, 14, 18, 20, 34, 40, 43–43, 45–49, 51–52, 60, 62, 67, 69–72, 76–79, 91, 97, 101, 103, 106–108, 110, 112, 120, 122–123, 126, 142, 145–146, 149, 154, 156–159
protestant, 28–29, 66, 90, 150

renunciation, 60–61 62, 64, 134, 151
repentance, 11, 31, 34, 36–37, 40, 43, 38, 51, 53, 57, 59, 76, 83–85, 96, 122, 135, 157
response, 22, 33, 52, 59, 60–61, 63, 68, 96, 99, 101, 106, 116–117, 134

Resurrection, 13, 17–18, 22–23, 30, 32, 39, 48–50, 62, 70, 85, 101–102, 105, 152

Schlink, Edmund, 99, 100
seal, 10, 24, 45, 48–49, 65, 67, 77–78, 107, 125, 137
sign of the cross, 5, 7–11, 18, 23, 26, 48–49, 66=67, 76, 106, 135, 157, 165
sign, significance, 9, 36, 49, 82–83, 85, 86–87, 129, 160
Small Catechism, 26, 28–29, 52, 73, 75, 82, 94
sponsors, 19–20, 41, 134–138
St. Bernard, 143
superstition, 7, 9, 62, 66, 76

Ten Commandments, 20, 127
The Doctrine of Baptism, 99
Thomas, Lewis, 105
total depravity, 56
Trinity, 44, 78, 143, 157, 178

unbaptized, 9, 11, 73, 80

welcome, the, 24, 149–153
Word (God's), 2, 19, 21–22, 24, 29, 32, 36, 40, 45, 50, 52, 56, 58–59, 64, 66, 68–69, 70, 72, 74–83, 85–87, 95, 100–101, 103, 110, 114, 117, 120, 126, 132, 134, 144, 151–53, 159, 160

Index of Biblical References

Matthew 19:13-15	93	Acts 11:16	36
Matthew 25:31 ff.	68	Acts 16:15	36
Matthew 28: 18-20	29, 33,	Acts 16:30	36
	114, 158	Acts 16:31	36
		Acts 16:33	37
Mark 1:1-10	45	Acts 18:8	37
Mark 10:14-16	73, 93, 100	Acts 19:5	37
Mark 10:39	31	Acts 22:12	15, 16, 80
Mark 16, 33	52	Acts 22:16	37, 80
Mark 16:15-16	32, 69, 71		
		Romans 5:12 ff.	83
Luke 18:15-17	93	Romans 6	85, 86
		Romans 6:1 ff.	85
John 3:3	81	Romans 6:3	37
John 3:5	80, 81	Romans 6:3-4	38
John 3:6	102	Romans 6:4	23, 87
John 4:1-2	32	Romans 6:5	87
		Romans 6:11	160
Acts 1:4-5	34	Romans 6:30	37
Acts 2:41	34	Romans 6:4	23, 87
Acts 2	45		
Acts 8:12	33, 38	I Corinthians 1:13	15, 17, 38
Acts 8:28	35	I Corinthians 7:14	93
Act 9:13	33	I Corinthians 12:12	39
Acts 9:18	35		
Acts 10:47-58	36	II Corinthians 1:21-23	45

Galatians 3:27	38	Colossians 2:12	23, 38, 94
Ephesians 1:13-14	45	Titus 3:5-8	52, 79, 80
Ephesians 4:4-5	39		
Ephesians 5:25-26	80, 81	I Peter 3:21	39, 53